SAVOUR THE
FLAVOUR

SAVOUR THE FLAVOUR

Creating healthy and delicious
meals without adding salt

Gillian Bridgewater

Foreword by
Derek Llewellyn-Jones

VIKING O'NEIL

Viking O'Neil
Penguin Books Australia Ltd
487 Maroondah Highway, PO Box 257
Ringwood, Victoria 3134, Australia
Penguin Books Ltd
Harmondsworth, Middlesex, England
Viking Penguin Inc.
40 West 23rd Street, New York, N.Y. 10010, U.S.A.
Penguin Books Canada Ltd
2801 John Street, Markham, Ontario, Canada L3R 1B4
Penguin Books (N.Z.) Ltd
182-190 Wairau Road, Auckland 10, New Zealand

Published by Penguin Books Australia Ltd 1988
Copyright © Gillian Bridgewater, 1988

Produced by Viking O'Neil
56 Claremont Street, South Yarra, Victoria 3141, Australia
A division of Penguin Books Australia Ltd

Typeset in Cheltenham Light by Bookset Pty Ltd, North Melbourne,
Victoria
Printed and bound in Australia by Australian Print Group, Victoria

Designed by Sandra Nobes
Illustrations by Lorraine Ellis
Cover photograph by Mike Fisher

National Library of Australia
Cataloguing-in-Publication data

Bridgewater, Gillian, 1940-   .
    Savour the flavour.

    Bibliography.
    Includes index.
    ISBN 0 670 90076 1.

    1. Salt-free diet – Recipes. I. Title.

641.5'632

FOREWORD

In the past fifteen years there has been a fall in mortality from coronary heart disease and a lesser fall in mortality from stroke. High blood pressure is a known cause of stroke and dietary salt is implicated in high blood pressure. The fall in the death rate may be due, first, to fewer middle-aged and elderly people developing cardiovascular disease and, secondly, to new medical technologies to treat people who have ischaemic heart disease or stroke.

Clearly it is better to prevent cardiovascular disease if possible. This implies that people should change their lifestyle and alter their diets.

Recommendations which will help prevent cardiovascular disease have been clearly stated by expert committees in several countries. They are remarkably similar. The recommendations are: to cease smoking tobacco; to take more exercise; to change dietary habits so that the person eats less saturated fats and less sugar; to increase consumption of complex carbohydrates and dietary fibre; to reduce alcohol intake; and to reduce consumption of salt.

Most Australians eat too much salt. Food which has a lower salt content need not lose its flavour. This book offers a wide variety of recipes which will help you enjoy eating foods with a lower sodium content.

DEREK LLEWELLYN-JONES

CONTENTS

NATIONAL HEALTH AND MEDICAL RESEARCH COUNCIL RECOMMENDATIONS

The National Health and Medical Research Council in its Report of the Working Party on Sodium in the Australian Diet *(National Health and Medical Research Council, Australian Government Publishing Service, Canberra, 1984) concluded that:*

- Populations with a sodium intake less than 50 mmol/day* have a very low incidence of hypertension and a low mortality from vascular disease.
- Japanese population groups who at present have the highest known sodium intake (greater than 300 mmol/day*) have a high incidence of hypertension and a high morbidity and mortality from (cerebro) vascular disease.
- The average sodium intake of groups of Australian adults varies from 130 to 200 mmol/day.* Certain individuals habitually consume more than 400 mmol/day.*'
- In Australia the overall incidence in adults of a level of blood pressure that reduces lifespan (systolic above 160 mm Hg and/or diastolic above 90 mm Hg) is over 20 per cent.
- Severe sodium restriction (less than 10 mmol/day*) effectively lowers blood pressure in people with severe hypertension.
- Moderate reduction of sodium intake in Western communities reduces blood pressure to the 'normal range' in many people with mild elevation of blood pressure.
- Individual susceptibility may be important.
- Sodium balance is important in certain other disorders but there is little evidence to suggest that high sodium intake causes these diseases.

The Council also stated that the major sources of sodium are:

- Sodium in processed foods, particularly staple foods such as bread, butter/margarine and cheese.
- Discretionary sodium defined as sodium added to food during preparation, cooking and at the table.
- Sodium chloride added in processing where 'saltiness' is a characteristic of the food, e.g. ham, olives, Marmite and Vegemite.

Finally, the Council recommended that:

- The community should be encouraged to reduce consumption of sodium. The aim should be to achieve a community sodium intake of under 100 mmol/day . . .*

The extracts reproduced above cover only sections of the concessions and recommendations.

*100 mmol sodium = 2.3 g sodium or approx. 6 g sodium chloride

ACKNOWLEDGEMENTS

My thanks go first of all to my mother, who taught me how to cook, and who suggested that I write a book. Then I must thank my husband, Peter, and my daughter, Celia, who sampled and commented upon a range of concoctions — not all of which appear in these pages. Peter also provided botanical information, as well as devising the herbal map of Australia.

Thanks are also due to Dr Trevor Beard, Chief Investigator of the Canberra Blood Pressure Trial, who educated me about hazards involved in adding salt to food. His enthusiasm, advice and encouragement have been invaluable. I would especially like to thank him for all his help and criticism during the preparation of this book and in particular to thank him for contributing most of the material for the Introduction.

Wendy Gray, Beryl Evans and Vicki Deakin, dietitians, assisted with the dietary information, and my thanks are due to them. Staff of the Low Sodium Advisory Service in Canberra and Wendy Morgan of the National Heart Foundation have made many useful suggestions. Barbara Craker and Kate Cox were among those who have sampled dishes and proffered suggestions: Heather and Brian Tilley sampled more than most. Kari Stunden also provided background music for the writing.

INTRODUCTION

WHAT IS ALL THIS ABOUT SALT AND SODIUM?

Is it necessary to add salt to food to give it flavour? I never asked myself this question until my husband, Peter, and I joined the Canberra Blood Pressure Trial in 1983. For twelve weeks of the Trial we ate only food free of added salt and other sodium-containing compounds. We also attended lectures and group discussions, and read the printed information handed out to participants, including the Commonwealth Department of Health's *Dietary Guidelines for Australians*, and so became interested in the health advantages of a no-added-sodium diet (often called a 'salt-free' or 'low-sodium' diet).

At the start of the Trial we were surprised to find, as were many other participants, that we were still consuming considerable quantities of sodium, although I had long since abandoned the use of salt in most of my cooking and no longer added it to food. Early morning urine samples gave clear evidence that we were excreting, and therefore eating, excess sodium.

Along with the rest of the participants whose blood pressure was normal at the start of the Trial, our blood pressure remained normal. We suffered no adverse effects from the change of diet. Some of those people on the Trial who had high blood pressure, experienced a drop in their blood pressure. They were overjoyed at the prospect of being able to abandon or reduce the medication they had been taking, in some cases, for years.

Of course, *people on medication for high blood pressure should not abandon or change their medication without consulting their own doctors.* They should always talk to their doctors before beginning a no-added-sodium diet.

Although Peter and I have normal blood pressure, the Trial

1
-

persuaded us that we should avoid altogether sodium that did not occur naturally in foods. What we were being encouraged to do was to abandon our familiar, unhealthy high-sodium diet and to make good use of all the natural foods available, without adding sodium to them. It was not long before we discovered that a no-added-sodium diet tasted better than a sodium-added diet.

We began to explore natural flavours in our foods and to experiment, trying to enhance flavours and combining foods in new ways. Having had great fun in the kitchen with these experiments, I wanted to share the results. Hence this book.

SO — WHAT ARE SALT AND SODIUM?

Salt is sodium chloride, and is composed of two chemical elements: sodium and chlorine. Many other compounds added to food also contain sodium: sodium bicarbonate, monosodium glutamate, sodium nitrite, sodium metabisulphite, sodium acetate, sodium citrate, sodium phosphate, and so on. Any ingredient named 'sodium' should be considered when assessing the daily sodium intake.

SODIUM AND HIGH BLOOD PRESSURE

According to a report of the National Health and Medical Research Council (NH&MRC) of Australia, 20 per cent of Australian adults have high blood pressure. In the older age-groups, the figure may be as high as 60 per cent. Over half the people who are retired are affected by high blood pressure. High blood pressure increases the risk of stroke and heart attacks, which are the major causes of death in Australia. Many people, also, are disabled by high blood pressure, heart disease and other diseases of the circulatory system.

Some peoples in the world add more salt and some add less salt to their food than Australians do, and the incidence of high blood pressure and death from stroke for them is correspondingly higher or lower than ours. High blood pressure is unknown in peoples (such as the New Guinea highlanders) who do not add salt to their food. In fact, they often show a slight fall in blood pressure with age, unlike our own situation. By contrast, the Japanese generally eat food that

2

contains much more salt than does Australian food, and they have a correspondingly higher incidence of death from stroke.

The evidence from population studies is sufficiently strong for the NH&MRC to be convinced that there is a correlation between sodium intake and high blood pressure and that the incidence of high blood pressure and death from vascular disease increases as salt intake increases. Indeed there is a general consensus in the international public health field that the level of sodium intake in the Western world is far too high, and that there is probably a connection between high-sodium intake and high blood pressure.

The long life of some people who have eaten large amounts of salt all their lives does not disprove the theory that high intake of sodium causes high blood pressure. Few would challenge that pollen causes hay fever on the grounds that only one of three people sitting in a garden sneezes. Similarly, high-sodium intake has variable effects! This illustrates what is really common knowledge — everyone has a different constitution.

Australians are inclined to believe that an increase in blood pressure is an inevitable part of ageing, and that it can best be controlled by medication. However, prevention is always better than cure, and since there is evidence that a cause of high blood pressure is too much sodium in the diet, we may be able to reduce the incidence of high blood pressure by reducing our sodium intake. A no-added-sodium diet will certainly help many people who already suffer from high blood pressure. Apart from sodium, stress, alcohol, and probably fat can affect blood pressure. A healthy lifestyle, including regular exercise, may help to protect against the increase in blood pressure.

HOW MUCH SODIUM DO WE NEED?

We need sodium in order to live. Almost all the food we eat contains sodium as a natural ingredient, and sodium that occurs naturally in food is not harmful. It is sodium in excess — the sodium that we *add* to food — that does the damage.

Most Australians, by adding sodium to food, probably consume 130–200 mmol/day, and some consume as much as 400 mmol/day (the millimole or mmol is a convenient scientific measure — 10 mmol of salt contains 10 mmol of sodium). This intake is too high, and the NH&MRC has recommended we try to reduce it to 40–100 mmol/day. Overseas, the story is the same, with the United States Public Health Service setting a goal of 50–100 mmol/day, and the World Health Organization (WHO) recommending 85 mmol/day.

People have not always added salt to their food, and if human evolution is represented by one day, we probably started to salt our food at 7 minutes to midnight. There have been only some 80 generations since the time of Christ, and maybe 100 since the earliest records of civilisation. This number of generations is too few, in biological terms, for great changes in our requirement for sodium to have occurred.

Cooking does not destroy sodium, so a balanced diet with a range of cooked or fresh foods every day should provide us with adequate sodium. I have been told that we actually need only 8.5 mmol/day, so there is no need to *add* salt.

People sometimes fear that they will become depleted of salt during sweating, but apparently salty sweat is unnatural. Runners in the Canberra Blood Pressure Trial noticed a change to less salty-tasting sweat. On the normal Western diet the sodium content of sweat may exceed 50 mmol/L, but on a low-sodium diet it often drops below 10 mmol/L. The Israeli Army stopped issuing salt tablets in 1961, even though the Army spends a lot of time in the desert. The Australian Army no longer issues salt tablets.

Salt is a traditional remedy for cramp caused by excessive sweating, but many of the people in the Canberra Blood Pressure Trial reported a relief from cramp on the low-sodium diet. Presumably, since the sweat was less salty than usual, less sodium than usual was lost through sweating.

HOW DO OUR BODIES COPE WITH EXCESS SODIUM?

On the usual Western diet, our bodies are working most of the time to dispose of unwanted sodium. Nature has provided us with excellent mechanisms for regulating sodium concentration, and under the influence of hormones the kidneys cope with disposal or conservation of sodium, as appropriate. An elevated blood pressure increases the sodium excretion rate and is one option available to the kidneys for dealing with an overload of sodium. It is believed that high blood pressure results from a strain being placed on these regulatory systems by excessive intake of sodium over many years. The common way to deal with high blood pressure is for the doctor to write a prescription for a diuretic, a drug that forces the kidney to eliminate the excess sodium more quickly. This usually lowers the blood pressure, and the patient is happy. However, it seems crazy to eat more sodium than one needs and then to take a drug to get rid of it! In 1984–85 the Australian population of 15 million people received over 9 million prescriptions for diuretics, at a cost of over $46 million. What a waste of money!

OTHER HEALTH-RELATED PROBLEMS

There is some evidence that excess sodium is also a factor in health problems other than those already mentioned.

Fluid retention. People who eat excess sodium have some fluid retention, and it is possible to lose up to 2 kilograms of water in the transition from the usual Western diet to the no-added-sodium diet. Some people can actually see the difference when they look at their ankles.

Menière's disease. People with this disease have attacks of giddiness and vomiting, accompanied by deafness and ringing in one ear. The cause is unknown, but the symptoms can be quite severe. A no-added-sodium diet brings about a great improvement.

Kidney stones. The commonest ingredient of kidney stones is calcium oxalate, and the people who form stones are often found to be excreting an excess of calcium in the urine. Calcium excretion reverts to normal on a lower sodium intake.

NO-ADDED-SODIUM DIET AND MEDICATION

People who avoid sodium may not need a diuretic. People who are already on medication for any reason should consult their doctors before they change their diets. At the very least the need for medication may change, and medical supervision is essential to avoid side-effects.

THE IMPORTANCE OF A BALANCED DIET

The Commonwealth Department of Health's publications *Dietary Guidelines for Australians* and *Towards Better Nutrition for Australians* recommend that as a nation we should reduce our fat intake from an estimated 38–40 per cent of our daily kilojoule intake to no more than 33 per cent. It is particularly important to avoid saturated fat and cholesterol.

In preparing the recipes for this book, I have avoided using fat and oil as much as possible. When I have felt that fat or oil is required for the flavour of the dish, I have usually recommended polyunsaturated, unsalted table margarine or oil, and have used only very small amounts. Butter, sour cream and coconut milk all contain saturated fats, but they add a great deal to the flavour of the dish in the few recipes where they are specified. If you are concerned about your saturated fat intake you can either substitute a similar ingredient (such as oil or yoghurt) or consider these dishes in the context of your total fat intake. You may also want to avoid the dishes containing prawns, squid, liver, kidneys, milk, low-sodium cheese or eggs.

A good plan is to consider your diet overall, so that you do not eat a succession of fatty foods at one meal or in one day. Keep a note of what you eat so that your fat intake is spread out over the week. If you want additional advice about dietary fat and how to reduce your intake, consult the National Heart Foundation.

CHANGING TO A FLAVOURSOME DIET AND AVOIDING SODIUM

Salt has always been a highly valued commodity. In the world before refrigeration, salt was the best preservative. Eventually we became accustomed to a high-salt diet, and began to prefer it, even though it overpowered many of the natural flavours of foods. It is now time to turn the clock back.

SODIUM OUT — FLAVOUR IN

Adapting to a diet based on flavoursome ingredients, instead of sodium, requires some adjustment in shopping, cooking and eating patterns. Here are some strategies that will help you make the change.

- Allow time for your palate to adjust and you will find that:
  after 1 week, flavoursome unsalted food is passable;
  after 1 month, it is palatable;
  after 6 months, it is preferable.
- Plan meals in advance. Fresh ingredients are full of flavour and free of added sodium. They are easy to use if meals are planned.
- Prepare for impromptu meals by freezing home-made items for emergency use. Do not rely on tinned or processed foods, as the 'tastiness' of these is often due to added sodium.
- Be flexible. Why restrict certain types of food to certain times of day? Try soup for breakfast or muesli for lunch.
- Try new foods and flavours.

AVOIDING SODIUM

- Forget to buy salt (it is easy to avoid if you don't have any in the house).
- Forget where the salt-shaker is (except when visitors ask for it).
- Forget to add salt to dishes where the lack is not easily detected (e.g. cakes, desserts).
- Avoid dishes where you would miss the salt. Boiled eggs seem to be the downfall of many a no-added-sodium enthusiast. Forget such dishes until you are thoroughly accustomed to your no-added-sodium diet.
- Never use ordinary baking powder or sodium bicarbonate. One way to begin a no-added-sodium diet is to avoid sodium compounds that your taste buds won't even miss, such as sodium bicarbonate. Other raising agents can be

used in its place: a potassium-based baking powder (see page 170); Salt Skip baking powder; Salt Skip self-raising flour; yeast.

- Never use monosodium glutamate.
- Avoid fast foods and, if possible, avoid dining out at traditional-style restaurants. Monosodium glutamate, sodium bicarbonate or salt will almost certainly have been used in the preparation of fast foods and restaurant foods.
- Choose, whenever possible, restaurants that serve low-salt dishes. If in doubt, choose simple dishes (e.g. grilled steak or fish, salads, baked potatoes) at a restaurant. Sodium is less likely to be added to these than to sauces, gravies, batters and such.
- DO NOT BUY any product whose ingredients include salt or other compounds containing the word 'sodium'. Products to be particularly wary of include:
  breads, cakes, biscuits;
  tinned vegetables, fish, meat;
  breakfast cereals (most contain salt, although a few unsalted ones are available);
  cheese, unless it is a low-sodium cheese;
  bacon, ham, salami and other processed meats (use cold home-cooked meat instead);
  sausages, unless they are free of added sodium;
  prepared sauces (make your own);
  convenience or processed foods (many contain more than one sodium compound).
- Use fresh ingredients. Fresh vegetables are easy to prepare and, unlike many tinned vegetables, are free of added sodium.
- Make the change to the no-added-sodium diet rapidly. The stricter you are, the sooner you will enjoy the natural flavours of food.
- If you want to make a gradual change, concentrate on one item of food at a time. Unsalted wholemeal bread is a good one to start with. Once you are accustomed to the new flavour, move to another type of food. Try avoiding processed meats, for example. Gradually work your way through more items until your diet is completely free of added sodium.

ADDING FLAVOUR

There are three main sources of flavour that can be added to foods instead of salt.

Essential oils. Essential oils are not oily in the sense that olive oil is oily, but are complex aromatic substances. They are found in plants, and are concentrated in herbs and spices. Information on herbs and spices is given on pages 15–28.

Cooking. Processes such as frying, roasting or baking not only brown the food, but also produce new substances, which enrich the flavour. One example is the caramelisation of sugar. Another is the roasting of coffee beans, nuts and meats. Think of the flavour changes that are brought about in a lump of dough when it is baked in the bread oven.

Flavoursome substances. Most fats, oils and proteins are tasteless, odourless and colourless in their pure state. The substances that exist with them and which add flavour are mostly pigments, known as carotenoids or chlorophylls, or substances belonging to the chemical groups, known as aldehydes, ketones or free fatty acids.

- Experimenting is fun. Try adding flavours to different dishes, and so find out which appeal most to you.
- Make stock (there are recipes in the Soups are Something Special section), and use these in soups, casseroles and gravies.
- Use lemons, vinegar, tomatoes or yoghurt to increase tartness.
- Use flavoured oils (e.g. olive oil, sesame oil) in dressings or to flavour frying oil.
- Try out a new herb or spice — flavour and variety galore! (Pages 15–28 will tell you more about herbs and spices.)

SALT AND SODIUM AT THE SUPERMARKET

Simply avoiding cooking salt and table salt is not enough. There are only two ways for us to ensure a no-added-sodium diet. One way is to *return to fresh foods*, and to do our own cooking, bottling and baking as our great-grandmothers did, but with one great advantage — the refrigerator and the deep freeze mean that we do not need to use salt as a preservative. The other way is to *read the labels* on all packaged and tinned foods and avoid all those that contain added sodium. Suitable foods are available in the supermarket, and more are coming.

The food industry uses sodium to control the moisture content and texture of food, but the main reasons for adding sodium to processed foods are to *preserve* them and give them *so-called 'flavour'*.

SODIUM AS A PRESERVATIVE

Until recently, salt was the best preservative. The word 'salami' derives from the Latin word for salt. Bacon, ham, anchovies, sauerkraut, pickles, olives, soy sauce and Vegemite all become superfluous for those returning to a no-added-sodium diet. Believe me, after four weeks or so, these foodstuffs taste so incredibly salty that you wonder why you ever liked them! After the three months of the Trial, I tried a ham sandwich: it was like eating a mouthful of pure salt!

SODIUM AS SO-CALLED 'FLAVOUR'

Surprisingly, flavour is something we appreciate mainly through our sense of smell. Before food reaches our mouths and also as we chew it, aromatic substances are released. These titillate our sense of smell and contribute greatly to our perception of flavour.

By contrast, salt has no smell, and we sense it only when it is actually in our mouths and in contact with taste buds. Similarly, acid, bitter and sweet substances are recognised by taste buds, rather than through our sense of smell.

Sodium is not essential for flavouring, and Coles New World supermarkets have begun to cater for those of us who like no-added-sodium food. They now stock no-added-sodium processed foods in their Farmland range. At the time of writing, the range already includes asparagus tips, green beans, beef and vegetable stew, beer nuts, beetroot sliced in vinegar, whole baby carrots, cashews, fish fingers, Irish stew, mixed nuts, toasted muesli, mushrooms sliced in butter sauce, whole champignon mushrooms, green peas, peanut butter (crunchy and smooth), roasted peanuts, potato crisps, Australian salmon, pink Canadian salmon, creamed sweet corn, sweet corn kernels, tomato juice in large cans and in 250 ml boxes with straws, tomato paste, tomato sauce (300 ml and 600 ml), whole peeled tomatoes, and chunk-style tuna.

Also at the time of writing, two brands of unsalted margarine (Becel and Sundew) are available nationally, and other manufacturers have introduced several brands of unsalted butter, each of which is local to one or two states. Edgells have introduced no-added-salt baked beans and spaghetti, and Edgells and Ardmona supply several varieties of unsalted tinned vegetables. Most supermarkets carry Seakist no-added-salt tinned Canadian pink salmon and King Oscar (imported) no-added-salt sardines. This list could be extended, and I have been told that many more no-added-salt products are in the pipeline.

Almost all vegetables in the deep-freeze cabinet have been frozen without added sodium.

CARE WITH STAPLE FOODS

Here are some details about common foodstuffs that contain added sodium and which are difficult to exclude from our diet.

Bread. Ordinary bread has a very high sodium content (250 mmol/kg). People who take sandwiches to work may obtain half their daily sodium intake from bread. 'Reduced-salt' bread contains 50–170 mmol/kg sodium to comply with food regulations. To be legally described as a 'low salt' bread, the sodium content must be reduced to 50 mmol/kg. 'No-added-salt' breads contain between 5 and 20 mmol/kg, depending on whether they contain added gluten, which has a fairly high sodium content due to the method of manufacture.

Breakfast cereals. If a packet of breakfast cereal lists salt as an ingredient, it usually contains a very large amount. Ordinary cornflakes have a sodium content of 430 mmol/kg. An exception is Kellogg's Sustain, which has a sodium content of only

11

43 mmol/kg, about the same as the natural sodium content of meat. Several brands of muesli, puffed wheat and ready wheats contain no added sodium, and home-made muesli and porridge can be made from rolled oats without salt (see pages 34–37).

Cheese. I find cheese hard to live without, but fortunately cheddar and gouda style cheeses can be made with low concentrations of salt. Such cheeses can be obtained from gourmet food shops. Potassium chloride seems to work particularly well as a salt substitute in cheese, but people on medication for high blood pressure or advanced kidney disease should ask their doctors whether they can take the extra potassium of low-salt cheeses. Unsalted ricotta and cottage cheeses are also available.

SODIUM CONTENT OF SOME COMMON FOODS

(Average daily need: 7–10 mmol sodium)

BREAKFAST	sodium mmol
cornflakes (av. serve 30 g)	15
bacon (1 rasher – 40 g)	35

LUNCH	sodium mmol
ham sandwich	30
meat pie	45
pizza (⅓ medium – 200 g)	102
bread (1 av. slice)	6.5
spring roll	58

SNACKS AND ODDMENTS	sodium mmol
crisps (salted – 25 g bag)	10
crumpet (1 average)	8.5
cheddar cheese (30 g)	15
blue vein/parmesan cheese (30 g)	24
self-raising flour (100 g)	31

DINNER	sodium mmol
table salt (1 teaspoon)	85
soy sauce (1 tablespoon)	60
tomato sauce (1 tablespoon – 25 g)	10
tinned soup (1 cup)	43
cheeseburger (av. value)	63
Chinese sweet and sour pork (av. restaurant serve – 250 g)	47

Source: Information compiled by Vicki Deakin, Low Sodium Advisory Service, Canberra.

FOOD LABELLING

A regulation now requires manufacturers to state the sodium and potassium content of all low-sodium foods. Ingredients used in the preparation of such foods must be unsalted (e.g. unsalted margarine). However, standard foods sold without any nutritional claim can still contain salted ingredients without any mention being made of the salt content of that ingredient.

Don't forget to look, among the list of ingredients, for other sodium compounds, such as sodium bicarbonate and monosodium glutamate, as well as salt. If you want to be scrupulous in your avoidance of all added sodium, arm yourself with a book that decodes the food additive codes and check labels for any additives containing sodium.

The regulations governing food labelling in Australia are being improved all the time, and what applies now may well be out-of-date by the time this book is published. If you want to know the latest regulations, obtain a copy of the NH&MRC Food Standards Code, published by the Australian Government Publishing Service (the version in the *Government Gazette* will be the most up-to-date). You can also telephone your state Health Department if you have a specific question.

HERBS AND SPICES

Herbs and spices are the source of aromatic and concentrated flavouring. As such they are of great importance in preparing appetising and tasty meals without adding sodium.

Herbs can be defined as flowering plants that are valued for their medicinal properties, flavour or scent. Many of the herbs we commonly use today have come from Mediterranean regions, and were highly valued by the Egyptians, Greeks and Romans. The once-wild plants were cultivated and later transported to other areas, where they were grown and tended and often used for medicinal purposes. All our culinary herbs are 'exotic'. The culinary possibilities of the native Australian flora still await exploration.

Mostly we make use of the leaves and stems of herb plants, but sometimes we use the seeds. Parsley and mint are among the most common herbs, but basil, dill, fennel, thyme, marjoram and chives are also often used.

The term 'spices' encompasses those pungent or aromatic flavourings that are derived from the bark, root (rhizome) or berries of certain plants or trees. They usually come to us dried, and often powdered. The plants that produce them are native to a wide area of Asia: China, India, Indonesia. Ginger is cultivated in Queensland, but I do not know of any other spice being grown in Australia. With our climate, spice trees might grow well in some areas, but backyard spice-growing seems not to have the same appeal as the home-growing of herbs.

Vegetables, also being of plant origin, are often closely related to herbs. The difference is that they are less aromatic, and we can and do eat them in larger quantities. Herbs tend to be so pungent that we use them only in small quantities, as flavourings. Vegetables are derived from almost any part of a plant: leaves, fruits, seeds, roots. They come originally from different parts of the world: capsicum, potatoes, tomatoes and sweetcorn from the Americas; cabbage, carrots and rice from

Asia. Nowadays, of course, most vegetables are grown all over the world.

Understanding some botanical terms is useful, especially if you are interested in knowing the parts of a plant from which a herb or spice is derived. Here is a short list, defining some of the terms I use in the charts.

ANNUAL	Plant living for one year only.
ARIL	Brightly coloured, fleshy coat of seed.
BIENNIAL	Plant living for two years, flowering, fruiting and perishing in the second year.
BERRY	Many-seeded, fleshy fruit.
FRUIT	Ripened ovary of the flower, enclosing seeds.
PERENNIAL	Plant living for many years.
RHIZOME	Root-like underground stem.
SEED	Plant embryo enclosed by protective coat.
STIGMA	A receptive surface for pollen grains at the end of a tiny stalk (the style) within a flower.
TUBER	Swollen underground stem, used for storage by plant.

HERBS AND SPICES

NAME	TYPE OF DISH	TIME OF ADDITION	PART USED	HOW TO OBTAIN	SPECIAL NOTES
ALLSPICE (PIMENTO)	soups sauces stuffings casseroles curry marinades chutneys porridge cakes	beginning	seeds	buy whole or as powder	not the same as 'mixed spice'
ANISEED	breads cakes biscuits	beginning	seeds	buy whole	
BASIL	salads soups sauces tomatoes capsicum eggplant	towards end of cooking	leaves	buy dried or grow (annual plant)	makes herbal tea
BAY	soups sauces casseroles marinades vegetables	beginning	leaves	buy dried or grow (perennial bush)	
CARAWAY	salads casseroles cabbage potatoes bread cakes biscuits	beginning	dried fruit (called seeds)	buy whole	
CARDAMOM	eggs curry porridge bread cakes	beginning	seeds	buy whole or as powder	

17

NAME	TYPE OF DISH	TIME OF ADDITION	PART USED	HOW TO OBTAIN	SPECIAL NOTES
CELERY SEEDS	salads soups casseroles beans vegetables	beginning	dried fruit (called seeds)	buy whole	
CHERVIL	soups sauces vegetables	towards end of cooking	leaves	grow (biennial plant)	use freely
CHILLI	soups sauces casseroles curry meat poultry beans pickles vegetables	beginning	dried fruit	buy fresh or dried, whole or as powder or grow (annual plant)	use with care
CHIVES	salads salad-dressing sandwiches dips sauces vegetables	beginning or use fresh in salads, etc.	leaves	buy dried or grow (perennial plant)	use freely
CINNAMON	soups sauces stuffing casseroles vegetables curry marinades porridge biscuits cakes	beginning	bark	buy as quills or powder	

NAME	TYPE OF DISH	TIME OF ADDITION	PART USED	HOW TO OBTAIN	SPECIAL NOTES
CLOVES	soups sauces casseroles curry beans marinades pickles desserts	beginning	dried flower buds	buy whole or as powder	use with care
CORIANDER SEEDS	dips soups sauces casseroles meat beans curry rice marinades	beginning	dried fruit (called seeds)	buy whole or as powder	use with cumin
CORIANDER LEAVES	salads soups sauces beans curry tomatoes	beginning	leaves	grow (biennial plant)	
CUMIN	soups sauces casseroles meat beans curry rice	beginning	dried fruit (called seeds)	buy whole or as powder	use with coriander
DILL SEEDS	salad-dressing dips soups potatoes fish pickles	beginning	dried fruit (called seeds)	buy whole or as powder or grow (annual plant)	

NAME	TYPE OF DISH	TIME OF ADDITION	PART USED	HOW TO OBTAIN	SPECIAL NOTES
DILL LEAVES	salads soups sauces fish vegetables	towards end of cooking or use fresh in salads, etc.	leaves	buy dried or grow (annual plant)	
FENNEL SEEDS	soups casseroles fish	beginning	dried fruit (called seeds)	buy whole or as powder or grow (perennial plant)	
FENNEL LEAVES	soups sauces fish	beginning	leaves	grow (perennial plant)	
FENUGREEK	fish curry	beginning	seeds	buy whole or as powder	can be bitter
GINGER	soups casseroles fish meat poultry vegetables curry biscuits desserts muesli	beginning	rhizome	buy as 'root' or powder or crystal-lised	blends with most savoury or sweet dishes
HORSE-RADISH	sauces for fish, beef chicken eggs	do not cook, add before serving	root	grow (perennial plant)	

NAME	TYPE OF DISH	TIME OF ADDITION	PART USED	HOW TO OBTAIN	SPECIAL NOTES
JUNIPER	soups pâtés sauces stuffings casseroles marinades	beginning	berries	buy whole	
LEMON BALM	salads eggs	beginning or use fresh in salads	leaves	grow (perennial plant)	makes herbal tea
LOVAGE	salads soups casseroles	towards end of cooking	leaves	grow (perennial plant)	
MACE	soups sauces vegetables curry cakes	beginning	aril (coating around nutmeg)	buy as blades or powder	can use instead of nutmeg
MARJORAM	salad-dressing soups sauces casseroles vegetables marinades eggs	towards end of cooking	leaves	buy dried or grow (perennial plant)	use with basil, oregano
MINT	salad-dressing sauces lamb vegetables marinades	beginning or use fresh in salad-dressings	leaves	buy dried or grow (perennial plant)	makes herbal tea

21

NAME	TYPE OF DISH	TIME OF ADDITION	PART USED	HOW TO OBTAIN	SPECIAL NOTES
MUSTARD	salad-dressing sauces vegetables curry beef eggs poultry pickles	do not cook, add before serving	seeds	buy whole or as powder	mix with water before use
NUTMEG	soups sauces stuffing vegetables casseroles curry poultry eggs cakes desserts	beginning	seed	buy whole or as powder	can use instead of mace
OREGANO	soups sauces casseroles marinades fish meat poultry	beginning	leaves	buy dried or grow (perennial plant)	use with basil, marjoram
PAPRIKA	salad-dressing dips soups casseroles beans curry marinades	beginning	dried fruit	buy as powder	can use in most savoury dishes

NAME	TYPE OF DISH	TIME OF ADDITION	PART USED	HOW TO OBTAIN	SPECIAL NOTES
PARSLEY	use in any type of savoury dish, including salads and sandwiches	beginning or use fresh in salads, etc.	leaves	buy fresh or dried or grow (biennial plant)	use freely
PEPPER (BLACK)	use in any type of savoury dish, including sandwiches	beginning	whole dried berries	buy whole or as powder	sharper flavour than white pepper
PEPPER (WHITE)	as black pepper	beginning	berries dried after flesh removed	buy whole or as powder	milder flavour than black pepper
PEPPER (RED/ CAYENNE)	soups sauces casseroles	beginning	ground dried fruit of red chilli without seeds	buy as powder	use with care
POPPY-SEEDS	curry poultry breads cakes	beginning	seeds	buy whole	use to thicken curries
ROSEMARY	soups sauces stuffing casseroles lamb marinades biscuits	beginning	leaves	buy dried or grow (perennial ever-green bush)	use with care

NAME	TYPE OF DISH	TIME OF ADDITION	PART USED	HOW TO OBTAIN	SPECIAL NOTES
SAFFRON	soups sauces rice biscuits cakes	beginning	dried stigmas of flower	buy as powder	use only a pinch
SAGE	soups stuffings casseroles vegetables marinades	beginning	leaves	buy dried or grow (perennial plant)	use with care
SALAD BURNET	salads sandwiches	use fresh	leaves	grow (perennial evergreen plant)	blends with other herbs
SAVORY	soups casseroles vegetables beans poultry eggs	beginning	leaves	grow (annual or perennial)	use with care
SESAME	beans poultry vegetables breads biscuits	beginning or as garnish	seeds	buy seeds, oil or paste (tahini)	oil used for flavour
SORREL	soups sauces fish eggs	beginning	leaves	grow (perennial plant)	imparts piquancy
STAR ANISE	vegetables meat poultry	beginning	dried fruit	buy whole	use in Chinese cookery

NAME	TYPE OF DISH	TIME OF ADDITION	PART USED	HOW TO OBTAIN	SPECIAL NOTES
TAMARIND	sauces casseroles curry	beginning	pulpy lining of pods	buy as compressed mass	imparts piquancy
TARRAGON	vinegar sauces stuffings vegetables marinades fish poultry	beginning	leaves	buy dried or grow (perennial plant)	use with care
THYME	soups sauces casseroles marinades vegetables	beginning	leaves	buy dried or grow (perennial plant)	use with care
TURMERIC	meat curry pickles	beginning	dried rhizome	buy as powder	
VANILLA	cakes desserts ice-cream	beginning	dried cured pods	buy pods, essence or as vanilla sugar	

WHAT HERBS AND SPICES TO USE

Here are suggestions for suitable herbs and spices to use in various types of dish. The list is not comprehensive, and is meant to be used only as a guide.

BEANS (pulses)	chilli • cloves • coriander • cumin • ginger • marjoram • oregano • paprika • savory • thyme
BISCUITS BREADS CAKES	allspice • aniseed • caraway • cardamom • cinnamon • ginger • mace • nutmeg • poppyseeds • rosemary • saffron • sesame seeds • vanilla
CASSEROLES	allspice • bay • caraway • cayenne pepper • chilli • celery seeds • cinnamon • cloves • coriander • cumin • fennel • ginger • juniper • lovage • marjoram • nutmeg • oregano • paprika • parsley • pepper • rosemary • sage • savory • thyme
CURRY	allspice • cardamom • chilli • cloves • cinnamon • coriander • cumin • fenugreek • ginger • mace • mustard • nutmeg • paprika • pepper • poppyseeds • tamarind • turmeric
DESSERTS	cinnamon • cloves • ginger • nutmeg • rose water • vanilla
EGGS	cardamom • horseradish • lemon balm • marjoram • paprika • parsley • mustard • nutmeg • savory • sorrel

FISH	cayenne pepper • dill • fennel • fenugreek • horseradish • ginger • mustard • oregano • parsley • pepper • sorrel • tarragon
MARINADES	allspice • bay • basil • cloves • cinnamon • coriander • ginger • juniper • marjoram • mint • oregano • parsley • pepper • rosemary • sage • tarragon • thyme
MEAT	cayenne pepper • chilli • cloves • ginger • marjoram • mint • mustard • nutmeg • oregano • paprika • pepper • rosemary • sage • savory • thyme
POTATOES RICE	caraway • coriander • cumin • dill • paprika • parsley • pepper • saffron
POULTRY	chilli • ginger • marjoram • mustard • nutmeg • oregano • paprika • parsley • pepper • poppyseeds • savory • tarragon • thyme
SALADS	basil • borage • caraway • chives • coriander leaves • dill leaves • lemon balm • lovage • nasturtium leaves • parsley • salad burnet
SALAD DRESSING	basil • caraway • chives • dill • lemon balm • lovage • marjoram • mint • mustard • pepper • tarragon • thyme
SANDWICHES	chives • nasturtium leaves • parsley • pepper • mustard • salad burnet

SOUPS	allspice • basil • celery seeds • chervil • chilli • chives • cinnamon • cloves • coriander • cumin • dill • ginger • juniper • lovage • mace • marjoram • nutmeg • oregano • paprika • parsley • pepper • rosemary • saffron • sage • savory • thyme
SAUCES	allspice • basil • bay • capers • cayenne pepper • chervil • chilli • chives • cinnamon • cloves • coriander • cumin • dill • fennel • ginger • horseradish • juniper • mace • marjoram • mint • mustard • nutmeg • oregano • paprika • pepper • parsley • rosemary • saffron • sorrel • tamarind • tarragon • thyme
STUFFINGS	allspice • cinnamon • ginger • juniper • nutmeg • rosemary • sage • tarragon • thyme
VEGETABLES	basil • bay • caraway • celery seeds • chervil • chilli • chives • cinnamon • ginger • mace • marjoram • mint • mustard • nutmeg • oregano • paprika • parsley • pepper • sage • sesame seeds • savory • tarragon • thyme

GROWING HERBS IN AUSTRALIA

Herbs are not native to Australia, but they can be grown in Australian gardens. Where conditions are similar to their native habitat they will grow well, and so it is possible to predict the ease with which certain families of herbs will grow in different regions. The map on the following page is a guide to herb-growing, and the categories in it are indicators of both herb growth potential and flavour potential. If you live in one of the favourable areas, such as Tasmania or southern coastal regions of the mainland (except along the Bight), your herbs should grow well, without requiring too much attention, and should develop superb flavour. If you live in central Australia, you will have an uphill battle on your hands, and may find it best to grow your herbs indoors. For more specific horticultural information you will find it best to consult a gardening handbook.

For those of you who prefer to have fresh herbs with minimal effort, it may be easier to buy them fresh from the market or greengrocer. Dried herbs are, of course, readily available in supermarkets or health food shops.

HERB-GROWING REGIONS OF AUSTRALIA

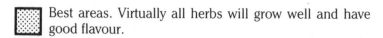 Best areas. Virtually all herbs will grow well and have good flavour.

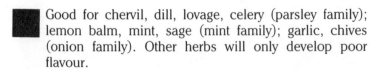 Good for chervil, dill, lovage, celery (parsley family); lemon balm, mint, sage (mint family); garlic, chives (onion family). Other herbs will only develop poor flavour.

Care and shade needed for chervil, dill, lovage, celery (parsley family); lemon balm, mint, sage (mint family). These herbs grow well: paprika and chilli (potato family), especially in the West; basil, marjoram, oregano, rosemary, thyme, savory (mint family).

Virtually all herbs grow well. Some never develop their best flavours, but are adequate: cumin, coriander, fennel, parsley (parsley family); basil, marjoram, oregano, rosemary, thyme, savory (mint family).

Good for most: frost can cause problems with some 'soft' herbs. Bay is especially good here; tarragon is cut by frosts.

All will grow, but need care and attention. Some are probably not worth attempting: chervil, dill, lovage, celery (parsley family); lemon balm, mint, sage (mint family).

Most will grow, but water needs to be watched in winter. Flavours do not match those of southern crops. Cumin and coriander do well. You might try more unusual herbs, e.g. lemon grass, or spices, e.g. ginger.

Marginal for most. Cumin and coriander do well, if watered.

Better to buy dried herbs, unless you are enthusiastic and persistent!

TO START THE
DAY

Commercially prepared breakfast cereals contain a surprisingly high amount of added salt. One or two varieties only are free of added salt. Home-made porridge or muesli, without added salt, provide the safest breakfast cereal.

BASIC MUESLI

When muesli is cheap and easy to make, why waste money on the packaged variety?

350 g (4 cups) rolled oats
50 g (1 cup) unprocessed bran
75 g (1 cup) wheatgerm
175 g (1 cup) dried fruit (sultanas, raisins, currants)
50 g (½ cup) nuts (slivered almonds, chopped hazelnuts)

Mix all the ingredients together and store in an airtight jar.

SPICED MUESLI

To the Basic Muesli recipe, add ½ teaspoon of cardamom and 1 teaspoon cinnamon.

MIXED CEREAL AND DRIED FRUIT MUESLI

350 g (4 cups) rolled oats
100 g (1 cup) rolled rye
75 g (1 cup) rolled barley
50 g (1 cup) unprocessed bran
75 g (1 cup) wheatgerm
2 tablespoons pinenuts

25 g (¼ cup) sunflower seeds
75 g (½ cup) sultanas
75 g (½ cup) raisins
50 g (½ cup) chopped dried apples
75 g (½ cup) chopped dried apricots

Mix all ingredients together and store in an airtight jar.

Variations
The three recipes above can be varied by using any of the following.
- different types of dried fruits, e.g. prunes, dates, figs, pears
- different types of nuts or seeds, e.g. walnuts, coconut, sesame seeds
- spices, e.g. ginger, nutmeg, allspice
- unsalted yeast powder

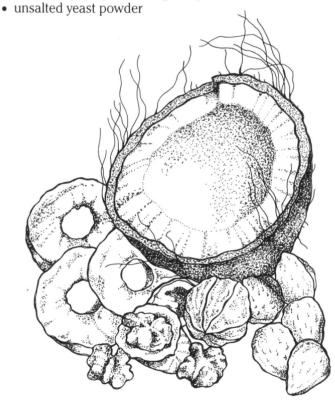

TOASTED MUESLI

100 g (1½ cups) prepared muesli (pp. 34–5)

1 tablespoon oil

1 tablespoon water

Mix all ingredients together and spread on a baking sheet. Bake for 1½ hours at 150°C, stirring several times to ensure even baking.

Note. Dried apples and dried apricots rapidly become crisp during baking. I prefer to add them after the muesli has been toasted.

Serve muesli
- with milk
- with raw or brown sugar
- with chopped fresh fruit
- soaked overnight in fresh orange juice
- with honey
- with fruit juice
- sprinkled with cardamom, cinnamon or ginger
- cooked like porridge
- with yoghurt

Uses of muesli
- breakfast dish
- healthy snack at any time of day
- dessert dish, served with fresh fruit and yoghurt

PORRIDGE

For each person allow:

25 g (⅓ cup) rolled oats

250 ml (1 cup) water

Cook according to directions for cooking on the oats' packet.

The following variations will give flavour so the salt will not be missed.

Variations

- stir in a pinch of cardamom and cinnamon
- stir in some sultanas
- stir in 1 teaspoon soft brown sugar
- substitute ⅓ cup milk for ⅓ cup water
- substitute other grains (e.g. polenta, semolina, oatmeal, rice flakes) for rolled oats

CONGEE

This breakfast dish is based on a Chinese method of cooking rice. Prolonged simmering allows rice to expand enormously, producing a large volume of congee. This can be prepared in advance and warmed up gently, with constant stirring to prevent sticking.

100 g (½ cup) brown rice
1½ litres (6 cups) water
500 ml (2 cups) milk OR more water
1 cm ginger root, peeled
225 g (1½ cups) chopped dried fruit (e.g. ½ cup each dried apricots, apples and sultanas)
1 tablespoon sunflower seeds

Simmer the rice in the water in a 3 litre saucepan for 3 hours. Add the other ingredients and simmer for 1 further hour. Serve with milk.

Serves 4

Variation

For the 225 g dried fruit, substitute ¼ cup sultanas, ¼ cup dried apples, 1 mashed banana and ¼ teaspoon nutmeg.

Remember that toast made from 'ordinary' bread is salted. Recipes for unsalted breads are in the section on Breads and Buns. Bara Brith, in particular, makes a pleasant toast.

YOGHURT

If you make your own yoghurt, you will have a delightfully sweet product, and you will know that it does not contain milk powder, which increases the sodium content. Yoghurt is easy to make, especially in summer.

500 ml (2 cups) milk

2 tablespoons natural yoghurt

Bring milk to simmering point. Remove from heat. Allow to cool, until the saucepan can be held comfortably in your hands. The milk is then at approximately blood heat.

Meanwhile, sterilise a glass bowl or jar by placing a metal spoon in it and then pouring in boiling water. The spoon will absorb some heat, and prevent the glass cracking. Discard water from the bowl, and allow the bowl to cool slightly.

Blend about ¼ cup of the warm milk and the natural yoghurt in the bowl. Stir in remaining milk. Cover and stand in a warm place for up to 24 hours. Refrigerate until required.

YOGHURT AND FRESH FRUIT

1 item of fruit (e.g. banana, apple, pear, peach)

250 ml (1 cup) natural yoghurt

soft brown sugar to taste

Peel or core fruit, as appropriate, then mash, grate or chop. Mix fruit, yoghurt and sugar together.

Serves 1

TOASTED GRAPEFRUIT

1 grapefruit

2 teaspoons brown sugar

Halve grapefruit and loosen segments in each half. Sprinkle with sugar. Toast under grill until grapefruit is warmed through. Serve immediately.

Serves 2

GRAPEFRUIT WITH FRUIT SAUCE

(contributed by Celia Bridgewater)

1 grapefruit, halved

25 g unsalted butter

2 teaspoons brown sugar

1 cooking apple, peeled, cored and grated

fresh juice of ½ orange

2 glacé cherries, for decoration

Remove and save segments of grapefruit. Remove and discard membranes of grapefruit. Fill empty grapefruit shells with grapefruit segments.

Simmer butter, sugar, apple and orange juice until apple is just soft (about 15 minutes). Pour over grapefruit. Decorate with a cherry and serve immediately while still warm.

For a dessert, stir 1 tablespoon brandy into the apple mixture.

Serves 2

Soups are ideal for breakfast, as they are warm, nutritious and rapidly reheated. Serve with unsalted toast, rolls or Crempog Las (see below). For stock and soup recipes see Soups Are Something Special.

CREMPOG LAS

Crempog Las is a Welsh form of unleavened bread, akin to damper or pocket bread. Served straight from the pan, it is as delicious an accompaniment for soup as any other hot, fresh bread.

200 g (1⅓ cups) plain flour
100 g (⅔ cup) wholemeal flour
pinch of mace OR nutmeg
a little oil for frying
2 eggs
4 tablespoons milk
1 tablespoon chopped parsley

Mix all ingredients together. Knead the dough on a floured surface until smooth (just a few minutes). Cut dough into 8 pieces and roll out each piece until it is as thin as possible. Fry each side of dough in lightly greased pan until each side is slightly browned, pressing down on the bread as it is cooking to ensure even cooking. Serve immediately, with or without unsalted butter. It can also be served with marmalade or honey.

Crempog Las can be prepared the previous day, stored in the refrigerator, and cooked quickly at breakfast time.

Serves 4–8

Be wary of using breadcrumbs, or any product rolled in breadcrumbs. Bread is salted, therefore bread-crumbs are too. Make your own breadcrumbs from unsalted bread, or use wholemeal flour, bran or oat-meal for coating meat, fish, etc.

FISH FINGERS

Fish mixture

500 g cooked fish
500 g cooked mashed potato
1 teaspoon chopped dill leaves
1 teaspoon lemon juice
white pepper to taste

For coating

1 beaten egg
coarse oatmeal, wholemeal flour OR salt-free breadcrumbs
1 tablespoon oil for frying

Combine fish mixture ingredients. Form into finger shapes or balls. Coat with egg and roll in oatmeal, flour or breadcrumbs. Fry until golden brown all over.

Serves 4

Sausages, bacon, packaged fish fingers and similar foods should be avoided at breakfast (or at any other time) because of the added sodium they contain.

PANCAKES

75 g (½ cup) plain flour
35 g (¼ cup) wholemeal flour
125 ml (½ cup) water
250 ml (1 cup) milk
1 egg
unsalted butter OR oil for frying

Mix first five ingredients together in blender. Heat a small knob of butter or a little oil in a frying pan. Pour in enough batter to cover the surface of the pan and fry gently until cooked. Turn pancake over and cook on other side until done.

Makes about 6 pancakes

Pancake fillings
1. 150 g cooked fish

150 g cooked brown rice

yoghurt to moisten

¼ teaspoon dill powder

pepper to taste

2. 2 tablespoons chopped, cooked chicken

1 tablespoon unsalted cottage cheese

paprika to taste

a few celery seeds

black pepper to taste

3. *2 tablespoons chopped, cooked chicken*
    1 teaspoon shallots or chives, chopped
    1 tablespoon unsalted cottage cheese
    pinch of paprika
    pinch of chilli powder
4. *½ apple, grated*
    2 teaspoons sultanas
    cinnamon to taste
    sugar to taste
    1 tablespoon yoghurt
5. *1 tablespoon fresh walnut halves, chopped*
    1 tablespoon unsalted cottage cheese
    1 tablespoon sultanas

Each filling serves 1

Orange glaze for pancakes
2 tablespoons cornflour

250 ml (1 cup) water

1 tablespoon sugar

juice of 1 orange

piece of orange peel

Dissolve cornflour in the water. Add other ingredients. Bring slowly to simmering, stirring all the time. Simmer until the sauce has thickened (a few minutes). Remove orange peel.

Serve as a glaze on pancakes filled with grated apple, sultanas and cinnamon.

Serves 4

KEDGEREE

500 g fish

450 g (2 cups) cooked brown rice

4 hard-boiled eggs, mashed

125 ml (½ cup) fish stock (p. 62)

1 tablespoon curry powder

125 ml (½ cup) yoghurt

Cook fish gently by simmering in 1½ litres water for 15 minutes, and retain the water for the stock.

Combine fish, rice, eggs and stock. Bake in 2 litre dish in pre-heated oven at 180°C for 15 minutes. Stir in curry powder and yoghurt. Bake for another 5 minutes in oven.

Serves 4

LIGHT MEALS

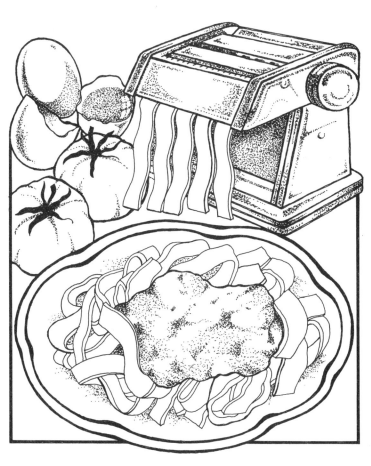

Taste buds are scattered over the surface of the tongue and soft palate. They are sensitive to four taste sensations — sweet, sour, salt and bitter. The absence of salt in a dish may be disguised by increasing the emphasis on one of the other three sensations of taste. Yoghurt, for example, is acidic and can be used to heighten flavours. Lemon juice, vinegar and tomatoes may also be used for this purpose.

CURRIED EGGS

2 hard-boiled eggs

3 teaspoons yoghurt

1 teaspoon curry powder

Shell eggs and slice in half, lengthwise. Scoop out yolks and mash in a bowl with yoghurt and curry powder. Fill whites of egg with curried yolk mixture.

Serve on a bed of lettuce, with slices of tomato or radish for garnish as a light lunch or dinner entrée.

Serves 1–2

CURRIED EGGS AND TOMATO

The flavour of the curry is best if it is prepared using individual spices. If these are not available, 2 tablespoons of curry powder can be substituted for them all.

4 hard-boiled eggs

1 onion, sliced

1 clove garlic

1 cm ginger root, chopped

¹/₄ teaspoon or less chilli powder

black pepper to taste

1 teaspoon turmeric

1 teaspoon cumin powder

1 teaspoon paprika

2 teaspoons coriander powder

1 × 400 g tin unsalted tomatoes OR 500 g fresh tomatoes, chopped

Shell eggs and chop into quarters. Simmer all ingredients, except eggs, together gently for 10 minutes. Add the chopped eggs. Simmer for a further 10 minutes. Serve with boiled rice.

Serves 2–4

OMELETTE WITH TOMATO, ONIONS AND POTATO

1 tablespoon oil OR unsalted butter for frying

1 onion, thinly sliced

1 tomato, thinly sliced

1 small cooked potato, mashed

4 eggs

2 tablespoons water

¹/₂ teaspoon basil

black pepper to taste

Heat oil or butter and fry the onion until just soft. Add the tomato and potato and continue frying gently for 5 minutes. Add more butter or oil, if necessary, to prevent sticking. Beat the eggs and water together. Add the basil and pepper. Pour the beaten egg mixture into the pan with the vegetables and cook gently until the eggs are set.

Serves 2

Salt is not added to food by people in such widely scattered parts of the world as New Guinea, South America and southern Africa. Among these people high blood pressure is unknown. Societies which use salt liberally, such as the Japanese, have a high incidence of high blood pressure. Absolute proof that salt causes high blood pressure is lacking, but the evidence is strong enough for the Australian Government to set the Recommended Dietary Intake at a much lower level than that consumed by most Australians.

CHEESE OMELETTE

¼ teaspoon mustard·powder
water to mix mustard
4 eggs
2 tablespoons water
100 g low-sodium cheese, grated
pepper to taste
¼ teaspoon paprika
⅛ teaspoon nutmeg

Mix mustard powder in water. Beat together the eggs and water. Stir in cheese, pepper, paprika, mustard and nutmeg. Pour mixture into a greased pie dish. Bake for 30 minutes at 150°C.

Serves 2

FISHY POTATOES

Herb butter and cheese give flavour to fish and potato. Presented in the potato shells, this can be an interesting lunch dish.

Per person
1 medium-sized potato

150 g cooked fish

1 tablespoon (25 g) low-sodium grated cheese

1 tablespoon (25 g) herb butter

Herb butter
2–4 teaspoons fresh, chopped herbs (e.g. parsley, chives, marjoram, basil, savory)

150 g unsalted butter

Prepare herb butter by mixing herbs into softened butter. Boil potato with skin intact for 20 minutes, or bake for 2 hours at 210°C. Reduce oven temperature or pre-heat to 180°C. Holding potato carefully, cut off top and scoop out flesh. Mash potato flesh and mix with fish and herb butter. Replace mixture in potato shell. Top with grated cheese and replace lid of potato. Wrap in foil and stand upright in an ovenproof dish. Place excess potato/fish mixture in a separate dish. Bake for 20 minutes at 180°C.

CHEESE AND TOMATO TOAST

¼ teaspoon mustard powder

water to dissolve mustard

2 slices unsalted bread

2 tablespoons unsalted tomato juice

50 g low-sodium cheese, sliced

Dissolve mustard powder in water. Allow to stand. Toast bread on one side. Turn toast over and pour tomato juice evenly over untoasted surface. Allow juice to soak in, adding more if necessary. Spread mustard over surface and cover with slices of cheese. Grill until cheese has melted and browned. Serve immediately.

Serves 1

Variation
Substitute chopped fresh or dried basil for mustard.

HOT HERB CHEESE LOAF

Try a slice of this herb cheese loaf with a bowl of steaming soup on a cold winter's day, or a slice of it with a salad for a light lunch.

150g (1 cup) wholemeal flour
150g (1 cup) plain flour
2 teaspoons potassium-based baking powder (p. 170)
1 teaspoon paprika
75g low-sodium cheese, grated
1 teaspoon onion powder OR 1 small onion, grated
1 tablespoon parsley, chopped
1 teaspoon basil
1 teaspoon marjoram
1 teaspoon thyme
1 egg
75ml (¼ cup) water
125ml (½ cup) milk
a sprinkle of extra herbs for decoration

Grease a loaf tin, and line base with greased paper. Mix all ingredients together in mixer for 3 minutes. Pour mixture into tin and sprinkle top with herbs. Bake at 180°C for 1 hour.

NOODLES AND QUICK TOMATO SAUCE

200g (2 cups) noodles
2 small onions, sliced
1 tablespoon olive oil
1 × 400g tin unsalted tomatoes OR 500g fresh tomatoes
1 clove garlic, whole
black pepper, to taste

Optional extras
1 shallot, sliced

½ green capsicum, sliced

10 green beans, sliced

¼ teaspoon basil

¼ teaspoon oregano

1 tablespoon bran

1 tablespoon burghul (cracked wheat)

1 bayleaf

Boil the noodles. Fry the onions in the olive oil, until golden. Add all the other ingredients and simmer gently for 20 minutes. Pour tomato sauce over drained noodles. Serve with a green salad. The tomato sauce can also be used with lamb chops, chicken or fish.

Serves 4

SAVOURY MINCE

1 onion, finely chopped

1 clove garlic, finely chopped

4 slices root ginger, peeled and finely chopped

1 tablespoon oil for frying

1 tablespoon curry powder

250 g topside mince

lemon juice to taste

Fry onion, garlic and ginger in oil until golden. Add the curry powder and fry for a few minutes more. Add the mince and fry until browned. Simmer gently for about 30 minutes. Squeeze lemon juice over mixture just before serving. Serve on toast (unsalted, of course) for breakfast or with rice for lunch.

Serves 2

Tinned baked beans usually contain added salt, and so should be avoided. Try preparing your own Spiced Beans with vegetables and spices.

SPICED BEANS

60 g (⅓ cup) haricot beans, soaked overnight and drained
50 g (⅓ cup) barley, soaked overnight and drained
1 small onion, sliced
1 clove garlic, sliced
1 carrot, sliced
1 stick celery, with leaves, sliced
1 choko, peeled, stoned and cubed
500 g fresh tomatoes OR 400 g tin unsalted tomatoes
½ teaspoon mace
½ teaspoon cloves
½ teaspoon ginger
125 ml (½ cup) water (if necessary)
1 tablespoon lemon juice

Simmer pre-soaked beans and barley for 1–1½ hours. Drain. Add all other ingredients, except lemon juice, and simmer gently for about 30 minutes, adding water if the beans appear to be too dry. Stir in lemon juice to taste.

Serves 4

CHICKEN, NOODLES AND SILVER BEET

200 g (2 cups) noodles
8 leaves and stalks silver beet, shredded
1 tablespoon oil OR unsalted butter for frying
200 g (1 cup) cooked chicken meat

2 tablespoons yoghurt

pepper to taste

Boil noodles for 10 minutes. Meanwhile, fry silver beet in oil or butter until it softens and green colour darkens. Shred chicken meat and stir into silver beet. Heat through. Strain noodles. Stir silver beet/chicken mixture and yoghurt into warm noodles. Season with pepper.

Serves 4

Salt, known chemically as sodium chloride, is one of many sodium-containing compounds added to foods. Others include sodium bicarbonate, sodium metabisulphite and monosodium glutamate. Once absorbed, the sodium portion of these compounds increases the concentration of sodium in the body. Normally, excess sodium is disposed of efficiently by the kidneys, but we can help our bodies maintain an appropriate concentration of sodium by reducing sodium intake.

To discover whether packaged foods contain added sodium — read labels.

CHICKEN, SAUSAGE AND RICE

50 g (½ cup) cooked chicken meat
100 g (½ cup) cooked brown rice
1 cooked unsalted sausage
1 tablespoon oil for frying
yoghurt to moisten
1 tablespoon poppyseeds
1 tablespoon chopped herbs (e.g. parsley, lovage, marjoram, oregano, basil)

You will need to search for a butcher or delicatessen that sells unsalted sausages, or make your own, so as to make this light lunch dish. Lightly fry chicken, rice and sausage together. Add other ingredients and heat through.

Serves 2

FISH PÂTÉ

1 × 95 g tin unsalted sandwich tuna

½ teaspoon fresh dill leaves, chopped, OR dill seed

white pepper to taste

juice ½ lemon

Purée all ingredients together in blender. Chill and serve with toast or biscuits. This is also suitable as a sandwich filling.

Serves 2

RINGED TUNA

1 × 185 g tin unsalted tuna

1 tablespoon unsalted tomato paste

6 tablespoons milk

¼ teaspoon basil

1 teaspoon paprika

1 tablespoon oil for frying

1 onion, chopped

150 g (1 cup) cooked brown rice

Simmer the tuna, tomato paste, milk and seasonings together. Fry the onions gently until golden. Add the rice and warm through.

Arrange rice and onion mixture in a ring on a serving plate. Heap the tuna mixture into the centre. Garnish with parsley. Serve with green salad.

Serves 2

BEEF AND SILVER BEET

½ teaspoon mustard powder

water to mix mustard

300 g (2 cups) cooked rice

1 tablespoon unsalted butter for frying

8 leaves and stalks silver beet

125 g (1 cup) cold roast beef, cut into thin strips

pepper to taste

Dissolve mustard in water. Leave while preparing rice, etc. Gently fry silver beet in melted butter, until beet softens and green colour darkens. Add rice and beef, and heat through. Add a little water if necessary, to prevent sticking. Remove from heat. Stir in mustard and pepper.

Serves 4

RISOTTO

250 g beef (e.g. round steak, with fat removed)

1 teaspoon thyme

1 teaspoon marjoram

4 tablespoons lemon juice

1 tablespoon oil

1 onion, sliced

1 clove garlic, sliced

225 g (1 cup) cooked brown rice

½ teaspoon caraway

1 teaspoon paprika

1 tablespoon unsalted tomato paste

4 tablespoons water

Cut beef into thin strips and marinate in herbs and 2 table-spoons lemon juice for a few hours. Fry beef strips, onion and garlic until meat is browned and onion golden. Add all other ingredients, including the marinade. Simmer 5 minutes. Add extra lemon juice if necessary. Serve with a salad at lunch.

Serves 3–4

RATATOUILLE RICE

1 tomato, sliced

1 small zucchini, sliced lengthwise in sticks

4 slices eggplant, cut across into sticks

1 small capsicum, cut into sticks

1 tablespoon parsley, chopped

pepper to taste

½ teaspoon cumin powder

½ teaspoon coriander powder

60 ml (¼ cup) water

225 g (1 cup) cooked brown rice

Place half the tomato, zucchini, eggplant, capsicum and parsley in a 2 litre greased casserole dish. Sprinkle half the quantity of each of the spices over the vegetables. Cover with the remainder of the vegetables and parsley. Sprinkle the remainder of the spices over them. Add a little water. Cover. Bake in a pre-heated oven at 180°C for 30 minutes or until the vegetables are cooked. Stir in the rice and reheat the mixture. Serve for lunch as a vegetarian dish, or as an accompaniment to light dishes such as omelette.

Serves 2

SOUPS ARE SOMETHING SPECIAL

If you are searching for a selection of simple dishes that are not only satisfying and savoury, but varied and versatile, then search no farther than this, the soup section.

Soups are simple and almost infallible. The basic essentials are a good stock and plenty of main ingredients. Add to these flavourings, thickeners and piquancy as necessary, and you have a delight to appeal to any appetite.

Stock cubes or stock powders are rich in sodium and should never be used as a basis for a soup, or added to a soup. To add stock cubes is to add salt.

STOCK

Stock is a basic ingredient for a good flavoursome soup, because it can give thickness and flavour.

Flavour is extracted from ingredients by simmering. It can be enhanced by frying or roasting the ingredients first. The browning process actually creates flavoursome substances. In a vegetable stock, *thickness* is produced by puréeing the vegetables after they have been softened by simmering. In a meat stock, thickness is produced by prolonged simmering of cartilage or gristly meat. Both are rich in the tough insoluble protein, collagen, which is broken down during cooking to gelatine, a simple, soluble protein.

Stock-making hints
- For a meaty soup, add gravy beef to marrow-bone stock.
- For a gelatinous stock, use cuts with plenty of cartilage (e.g. chicken wings, long marrow-bones).
- For a thick vegetable stock, include potato in the ingredients.
- For strongly flavoured chicken soup, use the carcass of a roast chicken, including as much of the remaining roast skin as possible. Alternatively, fry or roast chicken pieces before simmering.

- Avoid strongly flavoured herbs (e.g. tarragon, sage).
- Prepare stock in advance, so that it can be thoroughly chilled in the refrigerator, allowing the fat to set. Remove the fat from the chilled stock before making the soup.

Stock Preparation
Stock-making is simple. These are the basic steps:
1. Fry ingredients (optional).
2. Cover ingredients with water.
3. Simmer 1–3 hours.
4. Strain.
5. Strip bones of flesh and return flesh to stock (optional).
6. Purée vegetables (optional).
7. Discard bones, vegetable remains and herbs.
8. Cool stock to room temperature and then place in refrigerator for fat to solidify.
9. Remove fat from surface of stock.

MARROW-BONE STOCK

marrow-bones, sawn in pieces
3 litres (12 cups) water
2 sticks celery, with leaves, roughly chopped
2 carrots, whole
2 onions, whole
12 peppercorns
herbs (e.g. bayleaf, parsley, lovage, marjoram, thyme)
lemon peel (optional)

Cover marrow-bones with water and bring slowly to simmering point. Simmer for at least 2 hours. Add vegetables and peppercorns and simmer for another hour. Add herbs and lemon peel. Simmer for 30 minutes. Cool slightly and strain off vegetables, herbs and bones. Discard these. Chill thoroughly. Remove solidified fat from surface of stock.

Makes 2½ litres marrow-bone stock

FISH STOCK

head and bones of a large fish

2¼ litres (9 cups) water

12 peppercorns

1 clove of garlic

1 carrot, whole

1 onion, whole

1 bayleaf

Simmer all ingredients together for about 1 hour. Cool and strain. Discard bones, vegetables, etc.

Makes 2 litres fish stock

CHICKEN STOCK

Chicken flavour is strongest when chicken pieces are used on their own to make the stock. The addition of vegetables and herbs tends to obscure the chicken flavour. The richness of the chicken stock can be further enhanced by frying the chicken pieces before simmering them.

500g chicken pieces (see chart opposite) OR *carcass of chicken*

1¼ litres (5 cups) water

1 tablespoon oil OR *chicken fat (optional)*

Optional step: fry chicken pieces, turning them as necessary, until they are browned all over.

Simmer all ingredients for at least 1 hour. Cool slightly, then strain off the chicken pieces. Separate the meat from the skin and bones, and return the meat to the stock. Discard the skin and bones. Chill the stock thoroughly. Remove solidified fat from the surface of the stock.

Makes 1 litre jellied chicken stock

CHOOSING CHICKEN FOR STOCK

Different cuts of chicken yield different degrees of flavour and jelly and, of course, vary greatly in price. To determine which cuts are best in each respect, I experimented. The results are summarised in the chart below. The quantity of meat yielded by the different cuts also varies. You may find this information useful when considering which cuts to buy for making a casserole.

CHICKEN CHART

This chart shows the relative merits of different cuts of chicken for making stock or casseroles.					
Chicken portion	Economy	Jelly formation	Flavour	Meat/500 g original weight	No. of portions/ 500 g
carcass (1.5 kg bird)	★★★★★	★★★★★	★★★★	50 g	—
bones	★★★★	★★	★★	100 g	5
wings	★★	★★★★★	★★★	125 g	7
thighs	★★★	★★★	★★★★	150 g	4
backs	★★★★	★★★	★★★	150 g	8
giblets	★★	0	★★★★★	0	about 20
breast	0	★	★★★★★	225 g	2
drumsticks	★	★	★★★★	150 g	4

★ represents relative value on scale ranging from ★ (lowest value) to ★★★★★ (highest value).

VEGETABLE STOCK

Almost all vegetables can be used to make stock, provided no single flavour is dominant. The greater the variety of vegetables used, the richer and more general the flavour. Some herbs, such as marjoram and oregano, give a real boost to the stock, but others, such as thyme or sage, are too strong. Frying the vegetables gently before simmering increases the flavour, and is an optional extra step in the preparation of the stock. After experimenting with a number of vegetables I found the following combination satisfactory.

1½ litres (6 cups) water
1 carrot, washed and unpeeled
1 outer stick celery, with leaves
1 small turnip OR parsnip OR swede washed and unpeeled
2–3 leaves cabbage OR silver beet OR a few broccoli florets with leaves and stalk
1 onion, whole
20 peppercorns
1 bayleaf
½ teaspoon oregano
½ teaspoon marjoram

Roughly chop large ingredients into pieces to fit in the pan. Simmer all ingredients together until the vegetables are very soft (about 1 hour). Strain off the vegetables, and discard.

Unlike meat stock, vegetable stock is virtually fat-free, and does not need to be chilled and skimmed before use.

Makes 1½ litres vegetable stock

THICK VEGETABLE STOCK

Add a potato to vegetable stock recipe and simmer, as above. Strain off the vegetables and purée them with 1–2 cups of the stock. Return the puréed vegetables to the remaining stock.

Soups are substantial and satisfying, unless you skimp on the ingredients. A large bowl of a well-made soup can be a meal in itself. Soups are versatile. What could be better for breakfast or lunch, or more satisfying as a snack, than a bowl of thick, steaming, tasty soup?

ARTICHOKE SOUP

Jerusalem artichokes, like potatoes, are tubers or underground stems, used by the plant as storage organs. They are very flavoursome and, being easy to grow, are well worth planting in an odd corner of the garden.

500 g Jerusalem artichokes, scraped and chopped

1 large onion, sliced

1 clove garlic, chopped

1 tablespoon unsalted butter for frying

1 large potato, chopped

500 ml (2 cups) chicken OR vegetable stock (pp. 62, 64)

1 small leek, sliced

6 peppercorns

250 ml (1 cup) milk

lemon juice (optional)

Fry onion and garlic until soft and golden. Add artichokes, potato, stock, leek and peppercorns. Simmer until soft (about 30 minutes). Purée. Strain if desired. Add milk and reheat. Stir in lemon juice to taste.

Serves 4

BEEFY VEGETABLE SOUP

1 litre (4 cups) marrow-bone stock (p. 61)
1 carrot, sliced
2 stalks celery, with leaves, sliced
1 small onion, chopped
1 tablespoon unsalted tomato paste
1 tablespoon red lentils
1 teaspoon paprika
1 clove garlic, crushed

Simmer all ingredients together until vegetables are cooked (about 30 minutes).

This soup improves in flavour if you allow it to mature for 1–2 days. Reheat thoroughly before serving.

Serves 4

BROCCOLI SOUP

200 g broccoli, including leaves and stalk, cut in pieces
1 onion, sliced
1 clove garlic, sliced
6 thin slices of leek
1 tablespoon oil OR unsalted butter for frying
500 ml (2 cups) water OR vegetable stock (p. 64)
2 tablespoons cornflour, dissolved in a little milk
500 ml (2 cups) milk
pinch of nutmeg
cream OR yoghurt for serving

In a saucepan, fry onion, garlic and leek gently in oil until soft and golden. Add broccoli and stock. Bring to simmering point and simmer until broccoli is cooked (about 10 minutes).

Purée, and sieve if necessary. (Sometimes woody fibres from the broccoli stems resist being puréed.) Return to saucepan. Dilute dissolved cornflour with remainder of milk, and add nutmeg. Stir into soup. Reheat, stirring all the time to prevent the cornflour becoming lumpy. Serve with a swirl of cream or yoghurt.

Serves 4

BUG SOUP

4 Moreton Bay bugs, uncooked
water to cover bugs
1 onion, chopped
1 bulb fennel (not leaves), chopped
1 tablespoon olive oil for frying
4 cloves garlic, crushed
3 tablespoons unsalted tomato paste
1 sprig fresh thyme
1 bayleaf
¼ teaspoon dried basil
¼ teaspoon fennel seed
⅛ teaspoon white pepper
4 parsley sprigs
2 tablespoons lemon juice
¼ cup broken spaghetti (optional)

Cook bugs in boiling water for 3 minutes. Cool, remove and chop flesh. Fry onion and fennel in olive oil until soft and golden. Add all other ingredients, except lemon juice and spaghetti. Simmer for 30 minutes. Add lemon juice, cook 5 minutes more and serve. If desired, the broken spaghetti can be added 15 minutes before the end of cooking to give greater body to the soup.

Serves 6

CAULIFLOWER SOUP

In this recipe the rhubarb and the spices make an interesting contrast to the cauliflower without dominating it.

½ cauliflower (300 g), cut in chunks

50 g rhubarb, cut in short lengths

375 ml (1½ cups) water

250 ml (1 cup) milk

⅛ teaspoon nutmeg

⅛ teaspoon chilli powder

chopped parsley for decoration (optional)

Simmer cauliflower and rhubarb in water until both are soft (about 15 minutes). Purée. If necessary, thin the purée with some milk. Stir remainder of milk into the purée. Add nutmeg and chilli. Reheat. Garnish with chopped parsley, after serving in bowls.

Serves 3–4

CELERY SOUP

Celery leaves are rich in flavour, so do not waste them!

1 litre (4 cups) vegetable OR chicken stock (pp. 64, 62)

1 clove garlic, sliced

1 small onion, sliced

2 sticks celery, with leaves, sliced

6 peppercorns

pinch of savory OR thyme

1 tablespoon cooked rice

3 tablespoons yoghurt

Simmer all ingredients, except rice and yoghurt, together until celery is cooked but still firm (about 30 minutes). Add rice and simmer another 5 minutes. If it is for immediate use, allow to cool slightly, then stir in yoghurt. If preparing in advance, store without yoghurt added.

Serves 4

CELERIAC SOUP

Celeriac is a root vegetable, with the flavour of mild celery. As it has rather a rough surface, I find it easiest to cut it into quarters, then remove peel from each quarter.

1 celeriac root, quartered, peeled and sliced

1 small potato, sliced

1 small onion, sliced

1 clove garlic, sliced

1 stick celery, with leaves, sliced

2 Jerusalem artichokes, scraped and sliced

1 tablespoon oil for frying

500 ml (2 cups) chicken stock (p. 62)

¼ teaspoon aniseed (optional)

250 ml (1 cup) milk

250 ml (1 cup) yoghurt

Fry all the vegetables together gently in a covered pot for 10 minutes. Add the stock and aniseed, and simmer until the vegetables are soft (about 30 minutes). Purée and strain, to remove any coarse fibres. Reheat, stirring in milk and yoghurt.

Serves 4–5

CHICKEN AND GREEN BEAN SOUP

1 litre (4 cups) chicken stock (p. 62)

1 stick celery, with leaves, sliced

6 green beans, sliced

1 small onion, chopped

1 carrot, grated

2 sprigs savory OR thyme

2 tablespoons cooked rice

Simmer together in a saucepan all ingredients, except rice, until vegetables are tender (about 30 minutes). Add rice, reheat and serve.

This soup may be prepared in advance and reheated. Always reheat thoroughly.

Serves 4

CHICKEN DUMPLING SOUP

For soup

1 litre (4 cups) chicken stock (p. 62)

½ leek, sliced

1 stick celery, with leaves, sliced

2 cloves garlic, sliced

1 cm ginger root, peeled

12 black peppercorns

250 ml (1 cup) yoghurt (optional)

For dumplings

chicken meat from carcass

1 tablespoon fine oatmeal OR wholemeal flour

1 tablespoon paprika

¼ teaspoon nutmeg

1–1½ tablespoons beaten egg (less than 1 egg) for every 100 g chicken meat

To prepare dumplings
Mince or purée chicken meat, moistening with stock if necessary. When puréed, squeeze out excess moisture. Mix together chicken meat, oatmeal or flour and spices. Moisten with egg. Form into balls, about the size of half a teaspoon.

To prepare soup
Simmer vegetables, ginger and peppercorns in stock for 15 minutes. Drop balls into barely simmering soup. Simmer for 15 minutes. Stir in yoghurt if desired.
  This soup may be prepared in advance and reheated. Always reheat thoroughly.

Serves 4

CHICKEN AND NOODLE SOUP

This soup is delightfully easy to prepare. It is also very flavoursome, provided the basic stock is strongly flavoured.

1 litre (4 cups) chicken stock (p. 62)

chicken meat, as available from carcass

1 small carrot, finely grated

1 tablespoon parsley (optional)

½ teaspoon paprika

50 g (½ cup) vermicelli

Simmer all ingredients together for 5 minutes.

Serves 4

71

*T*inned or packet soups contain added salt, and often other sodium compounds. Avoid using such soups, even as a basis for a home-made soup. Use fresh ingredients and flavour them with herbs and spices.

CHICKEN AND VEGETABLE SOUP

1 litre (4 cups) chicken stock (p. 62)
chicken meat, as available from the chicken carcass
1 carrot, sliced
1 stick of celery, with leaves, sliced
herbs (optional: see below)
6 peppercorns
2 tablespoons cooked rice

Simmer all ingredients, except rice, together until the vegetables are cooked, but still firm (30 minutes). Add rice and reheat.

Serves 4

Variations
- Herbs: bayleaf, rosemary, lovage, tarragon, savory or marjoram (be cautious, most have a strong flavour).
- Garlic, onion, peas, corn, broccoli or green beans may be added to, or substituted for, other vegetables.
- Grate or chop carrot instead of slicing it.
- Lemon juice or yoghurt for additional tartness.
- Burghul (cracked wheat) or barley may be substituted for rice.
- Garnish with small cubes of low-sodium cheese, chopped parsley or croutons.

Soups are cheap. The cheapest cuts of a carcass (the skin and bones) make the best stocks. Throw away bones from a roast and you throw money in the bin! Other ingredients — vegetables, pulses (beans and lentils) and grains — are cheap too. Soups are easy. Take virtually any vegetable, combine it with others, throw in some herbs, and variety is endless.

CHICKEN AND CORN SOUP

As the predominant flavour of this soup is chicken, the stock used must have a good chicken flavour. Chicken thighs, backs or wings, or the carcass of a roast chicken, form a good basis for the stock (see chart, p. 63).

1½ litres (6 cups) chicken stock (p. 62)

chicken meat, as available from carcass

2 cm piece of ginger root, peeled

150 g (1½ cups) sweetcorn

150 g (1½ cups) peas

25 g (¼ cup) burghul (cracked wheat)

Add all ingredients to stock and simmer for 15 minutes. Remove ginger root before serving.

Serves 6

Variations
- Use 50 g (¼ cup) barley instead burghul. Simmer barley in stock at start for 20 minutes, then add other ingredients and simmer as above.
- Substitute green beans for peas.
- Add 2 teaspoons paprika.

73

CHICKEN AND GREEN VEGETABLE SOUP

1 litre (4 cups) chicken stock (p. 62)

chicken meat, as available from carcass

100 g (1 cup) cauliflower florets

100 g (1 cup) broccoli florets

50 g (½ cup) peas

1 tablespoon grated carrot

1 stick celery with leaves, chopped

2 shallots, chopped

2 tablespoons burghul

12 peppercorns

2 sprigs savory OR thyme

1 teaspoon marjoram

250 ml (1 cup) yoghurt (optional)

Simmer together all ingredients, except yoghurt, until cooked, but still firm (30 minutes). Remove savory or thyme sprigs. For a tangy soup, stir in yoghurt. Reheat and serve.

Serves 4–5

CUCUMBER SOUP

A light summer soup. Serve chilled.

2 cucumbers, peeled, deseeded and diced

1 tablespoon unsalted butter for frying

500 ml (2 cups) chicken OR vegetable stock (pp. 62, 64)

125 ml (½ cup) milk

2 cm piece of ginger root, peeled

1 tablespoon cornflour

milk to dissolve cornflour

125 ml (½ cup) yoghurt

Fry the cucumber gently in the butter until soft (15 minutes). Add stock, milk and ginger and simmer gently for 30 minutes. Remove ginger. Purée and sieve the soup. Thicken by adding dissolved cornflour, and stirring while reheating gently. Cool. Stir in yoghurt. Chill and serve.

Serves 3–4

CARAWAY SOUP

Caraway seeds give a distinctive flavour to this rich meat soup, which is thickened with tomato and potato.

1 litre (4 cups) marrow-bone stock (p. 61)

1 onion, sliced

1 clove garlic, sliced

1 carrot, sliced

250 g gravy beef, cubed

1 tablespoon oil for frying

2 teaspoons paprika

1 tablespoon tomato paste

¼ teaspoon caraway seeds

1 tablespoon rolled oats

1 potato, cubed

Fry onion, garlic, carrot and gravy beef until lightly browned. Add stock, paprika, tomato paste and caraway seeds and simmer for 2 hours. Add rolled oats and potatoes and simmer for another hour.

Serves 4–5

EGGPLANT SOUP

1 eggplant, sliced

2 zucchini, sliced

1 onion, sliced

1 clove garlic, sliced

1 tablespoon olive oil for frying

1 tablespoon curry powder

500 ml (2 cups) water

500 ml (2 cups) milk

Fry the vegetables gently in oil in a large saucepan until they are slightly soft (about 10 minutes). Stir in the curry powder, and fry for a few more minutes. Cover with water and simmer for 30 minutes. Purée. Stir in milk and reheat.

Serves 4

FAGGOT SOUP

100 g lamb's liver.

flour for coating

3 large onions, chopped

1 clove garlic, crushed

1 tablespoon oil for frying

1 litre (4 cups) water OR marrow-bone stock (p. 61)

1 teaspoon paprika

1 tablespoon unsalted tomato paste

1 blade of mace

6 black peppercorns

1 bayleaf

croutons (fried or baked cubes of unsalted bread)

chives and parsley, chopped, for garnish

Slice lamb's liver and dip in flour. Fry the liver, onion and garlic together gently until browned. Add water or stock and paprika, tomato paste, mace, peppercorns and bayleaf. Simmer until liver is cooked (30 minutes). Purée and sieve. Serve with croutons, chopped chives and parsley.

Serves 4

PARSNIP SOUP

1 parsnip, peeled and sliced

3 mushrooms, sliced

1 clove garlic, sliced

1 onion, sliced

1 tablespoon oil for frying

1½ litres (6 cups) chicken stock (p. 62)

½ teaspoon basil

Fry the parsnip, mushrooms, garlic and onion in the oil until the parsnip is browned and the mushrooms cooked. Add the stock. Simmer for 30 minutes. Add basil and simmer for 5 more minutes. Purée. Reheat before serving.

Serves 6

LEEK AND CELERY SOUP

Leek, celery and polenta blend well to make a thick and delicious soup.

1 litre (4 cups) chicken stock (p. 62)

1 leek, sliced

1 stick celery, with leaves, sliced .

2 tablespoons polenta (corn meal)

Simmer all ingredients together until the vegetables are cooked, but still firm (about 30 minutes).

Serves 4

77

FISHY SOUP

1 litre (4 cups) fish stock (p. 62)

1 onion, sliced

1 clove garlic, crushed

1 carrot, sliced

1 stick celery, with leaves, sliced

1 small potato, cubed

2 tablespoons parsley, chopped

½ teaspoon fennel seeds

1 cup yoghurt

Simmer together all ingredients, except yoghurt, until vegetables are cooked, but still firm (30 minutes). Stir in yoghurt. Reheat gently.

Serves 4

MINESTRONE

Last-minute soaking of beans can be done by covering the beans with water, bringing to boil and boiling rapidly for 2–3 minutes. Leave to soak from 45 minutes to 1 hour, before using as directed.

100 g (¾ cup) haricot beans, soaked overnight and drained

2 litres (8 cups) vegetable OR marrow-bone stock (pp. 64, 61)

2 cloves garlic, sliced

2 onions, sliced

2 sticks celery, with leaves, sliced

2 carrots, sliced

50 g (½ cup) noodles

¼ cabbage, shredded

1 small swede, cut in thin strips

2 small potatoes, cubed

6 sprigs parsley

12 black peppercorns

1 sprig savory OR thyme

pinch of oregano

low-sodium cheese, grated

Simmer pre-soaked beans in stock for 1 hour. Add all the other ingredients, except cheese, and simmer until vegetables are cooked, but still firm (about 30 minutes). Sprinkle with grated cheese and serve.

Serves 6–8

MUSHROOM SOUP

200 g mushrooms, whole

1 onion, sliced

1 tablespoon unsalted butter for frying

375 ml (1½ cups) vegetable OR chicken stock (pp. 64, 62)

375 ml (1½ cups) water

1 stick (50 g) rhubarb

250 ml (1 cup) milk

½ teaspoon basil

1 tablespoon cornflour dissolved in a little milk

Fry mushrooms and onion in butter. Add stock, water and rhubarb. Simmer 15 minutes, until rhubarb is soft. Purée. Cool and remove butter from surface. Stir in milk and basil. Reheat. Stir in cornflour dissolved in milk, stirring constantly to achieve a smooth consistency.

Serves 4

Soups store. Soups mature. Soups survive 3 days in the refrigerator — much longer in the freezer. Storage often improves flavour. Soups can be reheated in a few minutes, at any time, but they should always be thoroughly reheated, not just warmed up.

OXTAIL SOUP

1½ litres (6 cups) marrow-bone stock (p. 61)
1 oxtail
1 onion, sliced
1 carrot, sliced
1 small parsnip, chopped
1 stick celery, with leaves, sliced
12 juniper berries (optional)
12 peppercorns
1 bayleaf

Simmer all ingredients together for 3 hours. Remove pieces of oxtail. Take the meat off the bones and discard bones. Remove 2 cupfuls of the vegetables and stock and purée them. Return puréed vegetables and pieces of meat to soup. When cool, remove fat from the surface of the soup. Reheat thoroughly when required.

Serves 6

SPICY PUMPKIN SOUP

500 g pumpkin, cut in chunks
1 onion, chopped
1 clove garlic, chopped

¹/₄ teaspoon cinnamon

¹/₄ teaspoon nutmeg

1 litre (4 cups) vegetable stock (p. 64)

1 egg, beaten

1 cup yoghurt

chopped parsley for garnish

Simmer pumpkin, onion, garlic and spices in the stock until the pumpkin is cooked (about 30 minutes). Purée. Reheat, whisking in the beaten egg until it is cooked. Stir in yoghurt, reheat gently and serve, garnished with parsley.

Serves 5–6

SORREL SOUP

If you are fortunate enough to have sorrel growing in your garden, don't waste it, but make this soup occasionally. Your guests will find both the dark green colour, contrasting with yoghurt, and the flavour of the sorrel, with its slightly acidic tang, interesting. They are unlikely to guess the soup's main ingredient.

300 g sorrel leaves

3 large lettuce leaves

2 medium-sized potatoes, sliced

1 clove garlic, sliced

1 onion, sliced

1 litre (4 cups) vegetable stock (p. 64)

4 tablespoons yoghurt

Wash and shred sorrel and lettuce leaves. Add all ingredients except yoghurt to the stock and simmer for about 30 minutes, or until potatoes are cooked. Purée and reheat. Stir in yoghurt just before serving.

Serves 4

TOMATO SOUP WITH CORIANDER

Different varieties of tomato have different degrees of acidity. If the variety of tomato you have used is fairly neutral, and the finished soup lacks piquancy, add lemon juice.

1 kg tomatoes, roughly chopped
1 onion, sliced
1 clove garlic, sliced
1 carrot, sliced
1 stick celery, with leaves, sliced
1 tablespoon wholemeal flour
250 ml (1 cup) water OR *vegetable stock (p. 64)*
6 black peppercorns
1/2 teaspoon paprika
1/2 teaspoon cumin powder
1/2 teaspoon coriander powder

Simmer all ingredients together until the vegetables are cooked (about 1 hour). Purée and sieve. Reheat and serve, or serve chilled.

Serves 4

SPICY TOMATO SOUP

Garnish tomato soups with a swirl of cream or yoghurt, a sprinkling of chopped chives or parsley, croutons or a few chopped vegetables (e.g. diced carrot, cucumber or capsicum).

1 kg tomatoes, roughly chopped
1 onion, sliced

1 clove garlic, sliced

1 carrot, sliced

250 ml (1 cup) water OR vegetable stock (p. 64)

¼ teaspoon ginger

¼ teaspoon mace

6 whole cloves

1 tablespoon burghul (cracked wheat)

Simmer all ingredients together until vegetables are cooked (about 1 hour). Purée and sieve. Reheat and serve, or serve chilled.

Serves 4

POTATO AND LEEK SOUP

1 litre (4 cups) chicken stock (p. 62)

1 leek, sliced

1 potato (200 g), cubed

½ teaspoon dill seed

1 egg

1 teaspoon paprika

1 teaspoon mustard powder

Simmer stock, vegetables and dill together until the potatoes are cooked (about 30 minutes). Beat the egg and stir in the spices. Allow to stand for a few minutes. Stir the egg mixture into the simmering soup, whisking until the egg is set.

This soup improves in flavour if kept for a day or two. Store without egg mixture added. Always reheat thoroughly.

Serves 4

Variations
To vary the flavour slightly, add 100 g of Jerusalem artichokes, swede or sweet potato, chopped into small cubes.

SILVER BEET SOUP

1 onion, chopped

250 g silver beet, chopped

1 tablespoon oil for frying

1 litre (4 cups) boiling water

2 tablespoons red lentils

250 ml (1 cup) yoghurt

¼ teaspoon cumin powder

pinch of chilli powder

¼ teaspoon turmeric

yoghurt, for serving

Fry onions and silver beet gently until the onions are golden. Add water and lentils. Reheat and simmer gently for 10 minutes. Purée. Stir in 1 cup yoghurt, then spices. Reheat gently. Serve with a swirl of yoghurt on top of the soup.

Serves 4–5

MOROCCAN PUMPKIN SOUP

800 g pumpkin, cut in chunks

1 onion, sliced

1 clove garlic, chopped

1 leaf and stalk silver beet, sliced

1 stick celery, with leaves, sliced

1 litre (4 cups) vegetable OR chicken stock (pp. 64, 62)

½ teaspoon cumin powder

2 cm root ginger, peeled

½ teaspoon pepper

1 tablespoon semolina

1 tablespoon lemon juice

Simmer vegetables and spices in the stock until the pumpkin is cooked (about 30 minutes). Purée and reheat, stirring in the semolina to thicken the soup, as necessary. Stir in the lemon juice.

Serves 5–6

85

VEGETABLE SOUP

1 litre (4 cups) thick vegetable stock (p. 64)
2 carrots, sliced
1 stick celery, with leaves, sliced
½ leek, sliced
½ small swede, finely chopped
pinch of nutmeg
ground black pepper to taste
250 ml (1 cup) milk
1 tablespoon chopped parsley for garnish

Simmer all ingredients, except milk and parsley, together until vegetables are soft (about 30 minutes). Stir in milk and reheat. Garnish with parsley.

Serves 4–5

SUCCULENT
SEAFOOD IDEAS

I avoid buying cooked prawns because salt may have been used in their preparation. Avoid tinned prawns: they may be soaked in brine! Check the labels.

PRAWNS TANDOORI

10 large green prawns
1 clove garlic, crushed
3 cm piece root ginger, peeled and finely chopped
2 teaspoons cumin powder
2 teaspoons garam marsala
black pepper to taste
100 g unsalted butter
4 tablespoons yoghurt
5 tablespoons lemon juice

Cook prawns in boiling water for about 3 minutes, until they turn pink. When cool, remove flesh and leave whole or chop. Fry garlic, ginger and spices in butter for 2 or 3 minutes. Add prawns, yoghurt and lemon. Serve as an entrée with boiled brown rice.

Serves 4

AVOCADO, TOMATO AND PRAWNS

In this and the following recipe I have created two different, spicy, but unsalted dressings, which are suitable to serve with the popular combination of prawns and avocado.

8 large green prawns
2 ripe avocados, halved and with stone removed

Dressing

1 shallot, finely chopped
1 clove garlic, crushed
unsalted butter for frying
200 g tomatoes
¼ teaspoon allspice
¼ teaspoon cumin powder
black pepper to taste
1–2 tablespoons lemon juice
1–2 tablespoons sesame seeds

Cook prawns in boiling water for about 3 minutes, until they turn pink. When cool, remove flesh and slice.

While the prawns are cooking and cooling, pre-heat the oven and begin to prepare the sauce. Soften the shallot and garlic in the butter. Add tomatoes and spices and simmer for 30 minutes. Stir in lemon juice to taste and add the prawns. Spoon dressing into avocado halves, spreading the extra over the cut surface of the avocados. Sprinkle with sesame seeds. Bake, covered, in an ovenproof dish for 30 minutes at 180°C. Serve warm.

Serves 4

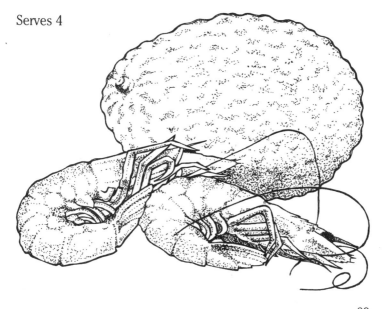

AVOCADO AND SPICED PRAWNS

8 large green prawns

2 avocados, with stone removed, peeled and chopped

4 large lettuce leaves

Dressing
a pinch of ginger

a pinch of black pepper

1 teaspoon lemon juice (optional)

a pinch of paprika

6 tablespoons yoghurt

Cook prawns in boiling water for about 3 minutes, until they turn pink. When cool, remove flesh and chop.

Mix all dressing ingredients together. Shred lettuce and place on individual plates. Place some of the chopped avocado and chopped prawns on the bed of lettuce. Top with a spoonful of dressing.

Serves 4

Variation
Halve and stone avocados. Combine prawns and dressing and spoon into avocado halves.

SQUID

2–3 squid

1 onion, chopped

1 clove garlic, crushed

1 tablespoon olive oil for frying

1 × 400 g tin unsalted tomatoes

1 tablespoon paprika

1 teaspoon oregano

1 teaspoon basil

8 peppercorns

To prepare squid

Grasp the head gently with one hand, and the body with the other and pull the two apart. The entrails will remain attached to the head and should be cut off and discarded. Make sure that the cartilaginous 'pen', which is attached internally along the length of the body wall, is also removed. Peel off the darkish thin skin that covers the body. Wash the body inside and out, and cut into strips or rings. Cut the tentacles off the head and cut them into pieces about 3 cm long. Discard the rest of the head.

To prepare sauce

Fry the onion, garlic and squid until the onion is golden. Add all the other ingredients, including the juice from the tin of tomatoes, and bring gently to simmering point. Simmer for about 15 minutes, or until the squid is tender.

To serve

Serve with boiled rice or noodles for main meal, or with pocket bread or toast for a snack or an entrée. An accompanying light green salad presents a pleasing colour contrast to the tomatoes.

MORETON BAY BUGS

(contributed by Peter Bridgewater)

4 Moreton Bay bug tails
175 g (3/4 cup) brown rice
2 cloves garlic, chopped
1 fennel bulb, chopped
1 tablespooon olive oil for frying
fennel leaves, chopped, for garnish

Cook bugs in boiling water for 3 minutes. When cool, remove flesh and dice. Boil rice and drain. Keep warm. Fry garlic and fennel in oil until soft. Add bug meat and fry for 1 minute. Mix fennel leaves with rice. Serve rice topped with bug and fennel mixture on individual plates. Serve as an entrée.

Serves 4

*S*odium is present in the fish, meat and vegetables we eat, for they, like us, are living things. Although sodium is necessary to maintain health, it is not necessary to add salt to food. The amount we require comes from a balanced diet of fresh food.

STIR-FRIED FISH

500 g fish
1 onion, sliced
1 clove garlic, finely chopped
1 cm root ginger, peeled and finely chopped
1–2 tablespoons oil for frying
2 tablespoons sesame seeds
¼ teaspoon fenugreek powder
black pepper to taste
½ fennel bulb, chopped
50 g (2 cups) bean sprouts
½ cup fennel leaves, chopped
1–2 tablespoons lemon juice
1 tablespoon cornflour
125 ml (½ cup) water

Shred fish or cut into small strips. In a wok, if possible, fry onion, garlic and ginger until soft. Add sesame seeds, fenugreek, pepper and chopped fennel and stir-fry for a few more minutes. Add fish and continue frying. Stir in bean sprouts, fennel leaves and lemon juice and fry for a further minute or two. Dissolve cornflour in water and then stir into mixture. Continue cooking until the cornflour has thickened. Serve with rice.

Serves 4

FISH CAKES

Fish mixture
400 g cooked fish

400 g mashed potato

½ teaspoon fenugreek powder

½ teaspoon paprika

½ teaspoon turmeric

For coating
beaten egg

wheatgerm OR oatmeal

1–2 tablespoons oil for frying

Mix all cake ingredients together. Form into flat cakes, each approximately 1 cm × 3–4 cm. Cover with beaten egg and coat with wheatgerm or oatmeal. Fry until golden on all sides.

Makes 18–19 cakes

GRILLED FISH WITH HERBS

To grill fish with herbs use, per person, 1 small whole fish, fish cutlet or fish fillet and prepare as in Baked Fish With Herbs (p. 94), wrapping each fish, or piece, in foil individually. Grill packaged fish for 7 minutes on each side.

BAKED FISH WITH HERBS

Fresh herbs are best for this recipe, but if these are not available, use dried herbs. Fresh herbs may be left whole, or chopped.

1 whole fish (e.g. bream, coral cod, snapper)

1 tablespoon lemon juice

black pepper to taste

1 tablespoon herbs (e.g. savory, thyme, oregano, marjoram, basil, parsley, dill, fennel, lovage)

Place fish on greased foil. Scatter herbs over fish and pour on lemon juice. Sprinkle with black pepper. Wrap foil to make a parcel, and bake in pre-heated oven at 100°C for 2 hours or 180°C for 1 hour (or until cooked).

Serves 4

MARINATED WHOLE FISH

1 large whole fish (e.g. snapper, bream)

a knob of unsalted butter

Marinade

1 tablespoon lemon juice

1 tablespoon oil

1 tablespoon chopped onion

1 clove garlic, crushed

1 teaspoon oregano

1 teaspoon marjoram

1 bayleaf, crushed

pinch of tarragon

1 teaspoon basil

1 tablespoon parsley

Mix marinade ingredients together. Score the surface of the fish and place in a dish. Pour marinade over fish and marinate for several hours, basting with marinade occasionally. Transfer fish to an ovenproof dish. Dob with butter or oil, and bake, covered, in a pre-heated oven at 180° C for 1 hour, or until tender.

Serves 4

COCONUT FISH

Use of a whole fresh chilli makes this dish 'hot'. For a milder dish, use just a pinch of chilli powder.

4 fish fillets

2 tablespoons lemon juice

1 cm root ginger, peeled and finely chopped

black pepper to taste

190 ml (¾ cup) coconut milk (see below)

50 g (½ cup) peas

2 shallots, chopped

1 teaspoon paprika

pinch of chilli powder OR 1 chilli, chopped

1 tablespoon poppy seeds

chives or shallot greens, for garnish

Cut fish into pieces about 1½ cm long and marinate in lemon juice, ginger and pepper for several hours, turning occasionally. Heat coconut milk to simmering point and add all other ingredients, including marinade. Simmer for 15 minutes or until fish is cooked. Serve in bowls, preferably Chinese, on a bed of brown rice, and sprinkle with chives or shallot greens.

Serves 4

Preparation of coconut milk

Coconut milk can be bought from gourmet shops or prepared by steeping 1 cup desiccated coconut in 1⅓ cup boiling water. Stand for a few minutes. Purée in blender and strain through muslin or sieve, squeezing or pressing to extract juice. Discard coconut.

FISH AND FENNEL

The delicate flavour of fennel seeps into the fish when it is cooked on a bed of fennel leaves.

1 onion, sliced

1 clove garlic, sliced

1 tablespoon oil for frying

4 stalks and leaves of fennel

4 small whole fish, fish cutlets or fish fillets

Fry onion and garlic gently in oil until golden. Meanwhile lay most of the fennel leaves in bottom of a greased baking dish (retain a few for garnish). Pre-heat the oven to required temperature. Lay fish on top of fennel leaves. Cover with fried onion and garlic. Cover dish. Bake at 100°C for 2 hours or 180°C for 30 minutes. Remove fish and onions, and serve with a sprig of fresh fennel for decoration.

Serves 4

FISH AND GINGER

500 g fish, cut into cubes

wholemeal flour for coating fish

2 onions, sliced

1 clove garlic, finely chopped

1 cm root ginger, peeled and finely chopped

1 tablespoon oil for frying

250 ml (1 cup) water

sprig of lovage (optional)

¼ teaspoon fennel powder

sprig of parsley

2 tablespoons lemon juice

Roll cubed fish in wholemeal flour until coated on all sides. Fry onion, garlic and ginger until soft. Add fish and fry lightly on all sides. Add water and herbs and simmer until cooked (about 15 minutes). Add lemon juice before serving. Serve with rice and decorate with sliced vegetables (e.g. tomato, cucumber and zucchini).

Serves 4

FISH KEBABS

500 g fish fillets (thick fleshy fish is best for this recipe)

Sauce

1 small onion, finely chopped

1 tablespoon oil for frying

¼ teaspoon fenugreek powder

¼ teaspoon cumin powder

¼ teaspoon turmeric

pinch of fennel powder

250 ml (1 cup) yoghurt

Cut fish into cubes and thread on bamboo skewers to form kebabs. Gently fry the onion until soft and golden. Add the spices and fry for a further 1–2 minutes. Stir in yoghurt, and warm through. Grill kebabs and pour sauce over them.

As a variation, omit the onion and stir spices into yoghurt.

Serves 4

ROSEMARY TROUT

1 trout per person

1 teaspoon rosemary leaves

black pepper to taste

Pre-heat the oven to the required temperature. Place trout in greased dish. Sprinkle with rosemary and pepper. Cover. Bake for 2 hours at 100°C, or for 30 minutes at 180°C. Serve with new potatoes.

SAUCES TO ACCOMPANY FISH

The following sauces can all be served with fillets of grilled or baked fish. Each of the following sauces serves 4.

Cucumber sauce

½ cucumber, peeled and thinly sliced

50 g unsalted butter

150 ml (⅔ cup) sour cream OR yoghurt

½ teaspoon chopped dill leaves (fresh, if possible)

Soften cucumber slices gently in butter for 15 minutes. Stir in sour cream or yoghurt and allow it to melt. Add dill.

As a variation you could fry the following ingredients together and add to the cucumber sauce:

1 clove garlic, finely chopped

4 thin slices ginger, peeled and finely chopped

1 small onion, finely chopped

Dill and lemon sauce

1½ tablespoons cornflour

250 ml (1 cup) milk

2 tablespoons lemon juice

2 teaspoons dill leaves, chopped (fresh, if possible)

white pepper to taste

pinch of chilli powder

Dissolve cornflour in a little milk. Heat remainder of milk to simmering. Stir into cornflour mixture, and return to pan. Reheat until sauce thickens, stirring constantly so that no lumps appear. Stir in lemon juice and dill. Season with pepper and chilli.

Sour cream sauce

1 small onion, finely chopped

1 clove garlic, chopped

2 teaspoons unsalted butter OR oil for frying

150 ml (⅔ cup) sour cream

white pepper to taste

4 tablespoons chopped parsley

Gently fry onion and garlic until soft. Stir in sour cream and reheat gently. Stir in parsley and pepper.

As a variation, you could add 1–2 teaspoons of curry powder after frying the onion and garlic, and fry gently for another minute. Omit parsley.

Sorrel sauce

Sorrel has a pleasant, slightly sharp taste, which complements
the flavour of fish. Grow some in your herb garden, so that you
always have it handy.

6 large sorrel leaves
4 lettuce leaves
1 onion, sliced
¼ cup (3 tablespoons) water
¼ cup (3 tablespoons) yoghurt
¼ teaspoon fenugreek powder

Chop sorrel and lettuce leaves. Simmer leaves and onion
together, covered, for 15 minutes, or until all are soft. Add
more water if necessary. Purée or mash with a fork. Stir in
yoghurt and fenugreek. Reheat gently, taking care not to over-
heat, as this will cause the yoghurt to curdle.

VERSATILE VEGETABLES AND RICE

*F*resh vegetables are fun! Fresh vegetables are easy! Fresh vegetables need no salt! Fresh vegetables are easy to cook.

Although the following recipes are for cooked vegetables, most vegetables are delicious when raw, and a bowl of chopped seasonal vegetables, without any dressing, is both colourful and appetising. Presenting the family with a range of raw vegetables in this way allows individuals to choose those they find most palatable. Fussy, but hungry, children will enjoy picking out the pieces they like the most, without feeling the pressure to eat vegetables because they are 'good for you'.

ZUCCHINI DELIGHT

1 medium zucchini
50 g unsalted cottage cheese
2 tablespoons yoghurt
1 tablespoon chopped onion
¼ teaspoon paprika
¼ teaspoon cinnamon
black pepper to taste
50 g (¼ cup) cooked rice

Blanch zucchini in boiling water for 5 minutes. Mix cheese, yoghurt, onion, spices, pepper and rice together. Slice the zucchini in half, lengthwise. Scoop out the flesh and chop it. Add zucchini flesh to cheese mixture and then fill zucchini shells with it. Bake at 180°C for 10 minutes to warm through.

Serves 2

EGGPLANT CASSEROLE

1 eggplant, sliced

1 onion, chopped

1 clove garlic

150 ml (⅔ cup) yoghurt

¼ teaspoon cumin powder

¼ teaspoon coriander powder

1 tomato, sliced

Steam the eggplant and onion for 10 minutes. Crush garlic into yoghurt and mix in the spices. Mix together eggplant, onion and tomato and stir in the yoghurt mixture. Place in an ovenproof dish. Cover and bake at 180°C for 30 minutes.

Serves 4

ZUCCHINI AND CINNAMON

Use olive oil to give the zucchini a fried flavour with a difference.

4 small zucchini, thinly sliced

1 tablespoon olive oil for frying

cinnamon to taste

black pepper to taste

2 tablespoons lemon juice

Fry the zucchini gently in the oil until lightly browned. Dust with the cinnamon and black pepper. Squeeze lemon juice over the zucchini slices and serve immediately.

Serves 4

*B*eware *of tinned vegetables. These usually contain a considerable amount of salt and should never be used. Some unsalted tinned vegetables (e.g. tomatoes, sweetcorn) are available. They are usually easy to identify, as 'No added salt' is blazoned across their labels.*

STUFFED ZUCCHINI

1 large zucchini
1 capsicum, sliced
1 onion, sliced
2 cloves garlic, sliced
1 tablespoon oil for frying
1 teaspoon coriander
1 tablespoon paprika
1 teaspoon cumin powder
pinch of chilli powder
2 tablespoons unsalted tomato paste
2 tablespoons water
325 g (1½ cups) cooked brown rice
1 carrot, grated
50 g low-sodium cheese, grated
1 hard-boiled egg, mashed

Blanch the zucchini in boiling water for 5 minutes. Cut zucchini in half, lengthwise. Scoop out the flesh and chop. Fry the capsicum, zucchini flesh, onion and garlic together for 5 minutes. Add the spices and fry for a further 5 minutes. Add the tomato paste, water, rice and carrot. Stir in cheese and egg. Place zucchini shells in a shallow, 2 litre, greased ovenproof dish and fill them with the tomato mixture. Bake, covered, in a pre-heated oven for 30 minutes at 180°C.

Serves 4

CORN AND COCONUT MILK

200 g (2 cups) corn

1 onion, sliced

1 stick celery, with leaves, chopped (optional)

60 ml (¼ cup) coconut milk (p. 95)

200 ml (¾ cup) chicken stock

½ teaspoon paprika

2 teaspoons cornflour dissolved in water

Simmer all ingredients together for 15 minutes until corn is cooked. (Make sure that the cornflour is properly dissolved before cooking.)

Serves 4

OKRA

This vegetable, which is occasionally on sale at the market, has a novelty value. Here is one way to prepare it.

1 onion, chopped

100 g (6–7 pods) okra, sliced

1 stick celery, with leaves, chopped

water

1 × 400 g tin unsalted tomatoes

1 small capsicum, sliced

1 clove garlic, chopped

¼ teaspoon oregano

Simmer all ingredients together for about 15 minutes, until okra is cooked.

Serves 3–4

Why not make rice and potatoes more than an accompaniment to the main meal? Make them a feature in themselves. Here are a few easy ways in which to brighten up your rice or potatoes, without adding salt.

CARAWAY POTATOES

This is a German method of baking potatoes, which I have adapted into a salt-free style. The method is very simple, and provides flavoursome potatoes to accompany a fairly plain meat dish.

4 medium-sized potatoes, scrubbed

1 teaspoon caraway seeds OR rosemary leaves

white pepper to taste

1 tablespoon oil

Scrub potatoes and cut them across in half. Arrange potatoes in baking dish, with cut surface uppermost. Brush cut surface with oil and sprinkle with caraway seeds or crumbled rosemary and pepper. (The quantity of caraway or rosemary used will depend on the size of the cut surface, and the degree of liking you have for the flavour.) Bake in a pre-heated oven at 200°C for 2 hours, or until cooked. Baste occasionally.

Serves 4

HUNGARIAN POTATOES

Another recipe based on a continental style of cooking potatoes.

2–3 large potatoes, scrubbed and thinly sliced

1 small onion, chopped

1 clove garlic, crushed

1 tablespoon oil for frying

125 ml (½ cup) water

1 teaspoon paprika

1 tablespoon unsalted tomato paste OR *2 tomatoes, sliced*

⅛ teaspoon caraway seeds

Pre-heat oven to 180°C. Place sliced potatoes in greased flameproof casserole. Fry onion and garlic in oil. Add water, paprika, tomato paste (or tomatoes) and caraway seeds. Simmer 1 minute. Pour tomato mixture over potatoes and bring back to simmering. Transfer to oven and bake for 15 minutes. Reduce temperature to 100°C and bake for a further 2 hours, or until cooked.

Serves 4

MICROCHIPS

1 potato per person

1 tablespoon oil

Wash potatoes and cut into very thin strips, like matchsticks. Soak the potato sticks for 30 minutes to remove sticky starch from surface. If you don't do this, the sticks are likely to congeal while cooking. Drain the potato sticks, and dab dry with kitchen paper. Roll the potato sticks in oil and then spread on a greased baking tray. Bake in a pre-heated oven at 210°C for 30 minutes, turning occasionally to ensure even cooking. A little bit of grated onion adds a nice flavour to this dish.

Why peel potatoes? If you leave the skins on, you benefit nutritionally, and you don't waste any of the flavour. All my potato recipes are for unpeeled potatoes — but the choice is yours.

JACKET POTATOES AND ACCOMPANIMENTS

Here is the basic method for baking potatoes in their jackets. Serve them with one of the accompaniments below if they form part of a simple meal, or alone to accompany a meal rich in gravy or sauce.

1 potato per person

squares of aluminium foil to wrap around potatoes

Wash and dry potatoes. Wrap potatoes in foil and bake for 2 hours at 210°C.

Herbs and cheese
1 tablespoon fresh chives OR parsley, chopped

4 tablespoons unsalted ricotta cheese OR sour cream

pepper to taste

Mix all ingredients together.

Herb butter
150 g unsalted butter

2–4 teaspoons fresh, chopped herbs (e.g. parsley, chives, lemon balm, marjoram, basil)

Soften the butter at room temperature. Mix in the herbs. Leave for at least 1 hour before serving. Store herb butter frozen in cubes for later use.

Curry sauce

1 small onion, finely chopped

1 clove garlic, chopped

1 tablespoon oil for frying

1–2 teaspoons curry powder

white pepper to taste

150 ml (²⁄₃ cup) yoghurt OR sour cream

Fry onion and garlic until soft. Add curry powder and pepper and fry for 1 minute. Stir in yoghurt or sour cream and reheat.

Spiced yoghurt

125 ml (¹⁄₂ cup) yoghurt

pinch of fenugreek powder

pinch of cumin powder

pinch of turmeric

Mix all ingredients together.

POTATO WITH MILK AND CHEESE

4 medium-sized potatoes, sliced

250–375 ml (1–1¹⁄₂ cups) milk

50 g low-sodium cheese, grated

Boil potatoes in milk, until soft. Mash potatoes and stir in most of the cheese. Place in a serving dish and sprinkle with remainder of cheese. Brown under grill.

Serves 4

MASHED POTATOES

4 medium-sized potatoes

1 clove garlic, crushed

1 onion, finely chopped

1/2 small leek, thinly sliced and finely chopped

1 tablespoon oil for frying

knob of unsalted butter for browning

Boil and mash potatoes. Meanwhile, fry garlic, onion and leek gently until soft and golden. Mix with potato. Form mixture into scoops, dot with butter and brown under grill.

Serves 4

CHICK PEA RATATOUILLE

150 g (1 cup) chick peas, soaked overnight and drained

1 large onion, sliced

2 cloves garlic, crushed

1 tablespoon oil for frying

1 medium eggplant, cubed

2 sticks celery and leaves, sliced

2 capsicums, sliced

1 medium zucchini, sliced

2 × 400 g tins unsalted tomatoes

1/2 teaspoon oregano

black pepper to taste

1/2 teaspoon basil

Simmer pre-soaked chick peas in fresh water for 1 hour. Drain. Fry onions and garlic gently in oil for 5 minutes. Add other vegetables, tomatoes, oregano and pepper, and simmer for 30 minutes. Add chick peas and basil, and continue cooking.for 15 minutes. Serve with boiled rice.

Serves 4–6

CHILLIED CHICK PEAS

2 × 400 g tins unsalted tomatoes
1 choko, peeled and chopped
1 onion, sliced
1 clove garlic, sliced
250 g (1½ cups) chick peas, soaked overnight and drained
1 blade lemon grass (optional)
¼ teaspoon chilli powder
½ teaspoon ginger
½ teaspoon nutmeg
½ teaspoon black pepper
juice of 2 teaspoons chopped tamarind pods (see below)

Simmer all ingredients together for about 1 hour, until the chick peas and choko are cooked. The mixture should have the consistency of a very thick soup. Serve with boiled brown rice and a crisp green salad.

Serves 4–5

Preparation of tamarind
Compressed (rather sticky) tamarind pods can be bought at health or gourmet food shops. Place the chopped pods in a cup and steep in enough hot water to just cover them. Strain the liquid into a bowl and discard the pods. Add the sour juice to the recipe. Prepared tamarind sauces are also available, but they may contain added sodium.

Cheese is a danger to those on low-sodium diets. Milk, from which cheese is made, has a high natural sodium content. The addition of large quantities of salt during the processing of cheese makes it a very salty food. Sometimes it is deceptively mild in flavour. A few low-sodium varieties of cheese are available from gourmet food shops, and can be used in moderation.

BEANY LASAGNE

75 g (½ cup) borlotti beans, soaked overnight and drained
1 small eggplant, cubed
1 capsicum, sliced
1 onion, sliced
1 clove garlic, sliced
50 g (1 cup) broccoli florets
1 × 400 g tin unsalted tomatoes OR 400 g fresh tomatoes
1 teaspoon oregano
1 teaspoon basil
6–8 sheets lasagne
50 g low-sodium cheese, grated

White sauce
1½ tablespoons cornflour
250 ml (1 cup) milk

To prepare bean mixture

Simmer the pre-soaked beans in fresh water for 1 hour. Drain and simmer them with the vegetables, tomatoes and herbs, except basil, for 30 minutes. A small amount of water may be needed if the sauce becomes too dry. Add the basil and simmer for 5 minutes.

To prepare white sauce

Dissolve cornflour in a little milk. Simmer remainder of the milk. Away from heat, stir milk into cornflour mixture. Return to pan and reheat, stirring constantly until sauce thickens.

To combine

In a 2 litre, greased ovenproof dish, spread alternate layers of beany mixture, lasagne, white sauce and grated cheese. Heat dish through for 30 minutes in a pre-heated oven at 180°C.

Serves 4

LENTIL AND EGG PIE

100 g (½ cup) burghul (cracked wheat), soaked ½ hour and drained
200 g (1 cup) red lentils, soaked ½ hour and drained
3 cloves garlic, crushed
2 teaspoons thyme
1 tablespoon oil for frying
4 hard-boiled eggs, mashed
125 ml (½ cup) yoghurt
black pepper to taste
100 g low-sodium cheese, grated

Simmer the pre-soaked burghul and lentils in fresh water for 15 minutes, and drain thoroughly. Fry the garlic and thyme in the oil until the garlic is golden. Add the burghul/lentil mixture, eggs, yoghurt and pepper and mix thoroughly. Place mixture in a 1½ or 2 litre, greased ovenproof dish. Sprinkle top with grated cheese. Bake in a pre-heated oven for about 30 minutes at 180°C. Brown the cheese topping under the grill. Serve with boiled brown rice.

Serves 4–6

LENTIL AND SILVER BEET PIE

1 onion, finely chopped
2 cloves garlic, finely chopped
150 g (3/4 cup) red lentils, soaked 1/2 hour and drained
125–190 ml (1/2–3/4 cup) water
6 leaves and stems silver beet, chopped
300 g (peeled weight) pumpkin OR swede, chopped
1/2 teaspoon nutmeg
black pepper to taste
2 medium potatoes, cooked and mashed
knob of salt-free margarine for browning

Gently simmer all ingredients, except potatoes and margarine, for about 20 minutes, until lentils and vegetables are soft. Cover with potato, dot with margarine and brown under grill.

Serves 4

PILAU RICE

1/2 teaspoon cumin seed
1 tablespoon oil for frying
100 g (1/2 cup) brown rice
375 ml (1 1/2 cups) water
1 carrot, sliced
1 potato, cubed
1 stick celery, with leaves, sliced
1 clove garlic, crushed
1 cm root ginger, peeled and finely chopped
1/2 teaspoon turmeric
1 teaspoon cumin powder
1 teaspoon coriander seed

¹/₄ teaspoon cayenne pepper

1 tablespoon lemon juice

Fry cumin seed in oil for a few minutes. Add rice and fry until the grain becomes opaque. Add water and simmer 20 minutes. Add vegetables and other spices. Simmer another 20–30 minutes, adding more water if necessary. Drain off any excess water and add lemon juice.

Serves 3–4

FRIED RICE

a few drops sesame oil

1 tablespoon oil for frying

1 onion, chopped

1 capsicum, chopped

1 stick celery, with leaves, chopped

1 tomato, thinly sliced

4 slices root ginger, peeled and finely chopped

325 g (1½ cups) cooked brown rice

Add the sesame oil to the frying oil and fry all vegetables, tomato and ginger until they are tender but still firm. Add rice and heat through.

Serves 4

FRIED RICE WITH MUSHROOMS

2 carrots, diced

1 onion, sliced

1 clove garlic, crushed

4 mushrooms, sliced

2 sticks celery, with leaves, sliced

1 tablespoon oil for frying

225–325 g (1–1½ cups) cooked brown rice

1 tablespoon lemon juice

1 teaspoon paprika

Fry the vegetables until cooked but still firm. Add rice and heat through. Add lemon juice and paprika and serve.

Serves 4

SPICED RICE

200 g (1 cup) brown rice

¼ teaspoon (or less) cinnamon

½ teaspoon ginger

1–2 tablespoons lemon juice

Boil rice for 15 minutes, or until cooked. Drain and stir in spices. Sprinkle with lemon juice.

Serves 4

Variation
Fry a sliced onion with the rice in a combination of peanut oil and sesame oil (a few drops only). Add boiling water and proceed as above.

CORIANDER RICE

8 slices root ginger, peeled and finely chopped

1 clove garlic, sliced

1 onion, sliced

200 g (1 cup) brown rice

1 tablespoon oil for frying

250 ml (1 cup) water

½ teaspoon coriander seeds

½ teaspoon cumin seeds

4 tomatoes, sliced

125 ml (½ cup) yoghurt

Fry ginger, garlic, onion and rice together until the rice becomes opaque. Add water to cover, and coriander and cumin. Simmer 30 minutes. Add tomato and simmer for a further 20 minutes. Drain, and dry off slightly in oven. Top with yoghurt.

Serves 4

SEVERI

a few drops of sesame oil
1 tablespoon oil for frying
1 capsicum, sliced
50 g (1 cup) broccoli florets
1 stick celery, with leaves, sliced
1 carrot, sliced or cubed
1 tablespoon sesame seeds
225 g (1 cup) cooked brown and white rice
2 tablespoons yoghurt
½ teaspoon tahini

Add sesame oil to frying oil and gently fry vegetables until they are tender but still firm. Add sesame seeds and fry for a further minute. Add rice and mix thoroughly. Stir in yoghurt and tahini.

Serves 4

MAINSTAY MEAT
AND CHICKEN

Add flavour to main meals instead of salt! You can do this by your choice of ingredients and by the way you cook them.

Ingredients
- *Main ingredients (vegetables, meats, grains, etc.) have individual flavours. Use plenty of these ingredients to make the dish thick and flavoursome.*
- *Herbs and spices have strong flavours. Use them to complement the flavours of the main ingredients, but use them sparingly.*
- *Use yoghurt or coconut milk to give a dish a creamy texture.*
- *Use the acidity of lemon juice, yoghurt, vinegar, tamarind or tomatoes to give a dish tartness.*
- *Use flavoursome oils (e.g. olive oil, sesame oil) in dressings or add to frying oil.*

Cooking
- *Marinate meats to impregnate them with flavour.*
- *Use slow cooking at low temperatures (e.g. in crockpot) to retain flavours and allow them to blend.*
- *Make the most of browning of foods. For example, top a dish with grated cheese (low-sodium, of course), and grill it.*
- *Prepare casseroles in advance and allow a day for them to mature. A dish is more flavoursome if the flavours have had a chance to blend in this way.*

'HOT' BEEF KEBABS

500 g topside, cut into small cubes, fat removed

Marinade
2 tablespoons lemon juice

2 tablespoons oil

½ teaspoon mustard

¼ teaspoon nutmeg

½ teaspoon paprika

¼ teaspoon ginger

¼ teaspoon black pepper

¼ teaspoon (or less) chilli powder

Sauce
1 × 400 g tin unsalted tomatoes

1 onion, sliced

1 clove garlic, crushed

juice of 1 tablespoon chopped tamarind pods (p. 111)

¼ teaspoon ginger

¼ teaspoon black pepper

¼ teaspoon nutmeg

1 teaspoon paprika

pinch of chilli powder

Combine marinade ingredients and meat cubes for several hours, turning occasionally. When ready to prepare meal, skewer the meat cubes onto bamboo skewers, and grill. While meat is marinating, prepare sauce by simmering all sauce ingredients together for about 30 minutes. For a smooth sauce, purée it. Reheat and pour over kebabs, when cooked. Serve with rice and Smooth and Crunchy Salad (p. 148).

Serves 4

Our bodies cannot tolerate too much sodium, and they rigorously control the sodium level at exactly the concentration needed to sustain life. The extra sodium in the Western diet increases the kidneys' workload, and a substantial body of research points to the kidneys as the prime agents in raising the blood pressure in response to this overload (more salt can be excreted at higher pressures).

MARINATED BEEF (KEBABS, BARBECUED OR GRILLED STEAK)

500 g lean beef, fat removed

Marinade
2 tablespoons lemon juice

2 tablespoons oil

1 tablespoon chopped mixed herbs (e.g. parsley, basil, oregano, marjoram, thyme, lemon balm)

1 bayleaf

1 clove of garlic, chopped

1 tablespoon unsalted tomato paste

Cut beef into appropriate-sized pieces: cubes for kebabs, larger pieces for barbecuing or grilling. Mix all marinade ingredients together in a bowl. Add the beef and coat with the marinade. Cover and leave for several hours, turning the beef in the marinade at intervals. Barbecue, grill or fry the meat as desired.

Serves 4

KOFTA

Meat balls

500 g minced topside
2 small onions
2 cloves garlic
1 teaspoon coriander powder
1 teaspoon cumin powder
½ teaspoon turmeric
⅛–¼ teaspoon chilli powder
¼ teaspoon black pepper
½ teaspoon grated lemon rind
½ teaspoon ginger
1 tablespoon wholemeal flour

Sauce

2 cloves garlic, finely chopped
6 thin slices root ginger, peeled and thinly sliced
1 × 450 g tin unsalted tomatoes
juice of 1 teaspoon chopped tamarind pods (p. 111)

To prepare meat balls

Mince onion and garlic. Then mix all ingredients together and form into balls.

To prepare sauce

Gently simmer all sauce ingredients until cooked (about 20 minutes). Purée and reheat. Drop meat balls into sauce and simmer for a further 20 minutes or until the sauce has thickened.

Serves 4

GOULASH

You can make this traditional Hungarian dish flavoursome by using a well-flavoured stock, and by long slow cooking. Use gravy beef, which contains a considerable amount of gristle. Gristle is rich in collagen, a tough protein, which is converted to soft gelatine by prolonged cooking. The result is a thick and tasty gravy, and tender meat.

500 g gravy beef, cubed, fat removed
2 onions, sliced
3 cloves garlic, sliced
1 tablespoon oil for frying
500 ml (4 cups) marrow-bone stock (p. 61)
1 carrot, sliced
1 tablespoon wholemeal flour
1 tablespoon paprika
2 tablespoons unsalted tomato paste
3 potatoes, cubed
¼ teaspoon caraway seeds

Fry meat, onions and garlic until lightly browned. Add all other ingredients, except potatoes and caraway seeds. Bring to simmering point and bake in the oven at 100–150°C for at least 5 hours. Add potatoes and caraway seeds and return to oven for another 2 hours.

Seves 4–5

EASY MEAT STEW

More acceptable to children than spicy casseroles, this stew can be varied by adding carrot, celery, swede or peas.

500 g blade steak, cubed, fat removed

wholemeal flour OR oatmeal for coating

knob of unsalted butter

·1 tablespoon oil

1 onion, sliced

250 ml (1 cup) water OR stock

2 tablespoons parsley, chopped

1 teaspoon dried yeast

Roll cubed steak in flour or oatmeal, then fry in butter and oil until well browned on all sides. Add onion and fry until golden. Add water or stock. Simmer gently for 1 hour. Stir in yeast and parsley. Serve with noodles.

Serves 3–4

SPICY CASSEROLE

500 g skirt steak, cubed, fat removed

1 large onion, sliced

2 cloves garlic, finely chopped

2 carrots, cubed

1 swede (about 300 g), cubed

2 sticks celery, with leaves, sliced

2 × 400 g tins unsalted tomatoes

1 bayleaf

1 teaspoon allspice

2 teaspoons paprika

black pepper to taste

Gently simmer all ingredients together for 1–2 hours.

Serves 4–6

MEAT AND POTATO CURRY

The potatoes, banana and tomatoes create a rich gravy for this curry.

500 g round steak, cubed, fat removed
1 onion sliced
1 tablespoon oil for frying
1 teaspoon paprika
1 teaspoon turmeric
2 teaspoons coriander powder
black pepper to taste
1 teaspoon cumin powder or seeds
¼ teaspoon chilli powder
3 cloves garlic, crushed
2 cm root ginger, peeled and finely chopped
4 medium-sized potatoes, cubed
3 tomatoes, thinly sliced
250–375 ml (1–1½ cups) water
1 small banana
1 tablespoon poppyseeds
2 tablespoons lemon juice
125 ml (½ cup) yoghurt

Fry onion until golden. Add spices, garlic and ginger and fry for a further 3–4 minutes. Add all the other ingredients, except the yoghurt and lemon juice, and simmer for at least 1 hour, or cook in oven at 100°C for 3 hours. Add more water if necessary. Just before serving, stir in the lemon juice and yoghurt and simmer for another 5 minutes. Serve with boiled brown rice.

Serves 4

*P*repared frozen foods are likely to contain salt and/
or other sodium compounds. Pastries and gravies
usually have salt added. Cheese is salted, so products
containing cheese (e.g. pizza) are very salty. Crumbed
items (e.g. fish fingers) have salt in the breadcrumbs,
apart from any other additive. Check labels.

SPICED MINCE AND LENTILS

500g minced topside
50g (¼ cup) chick peas, soaked overnight and drained
50g (¼ cup) lentils, soaked ½ hour and drained
1 onion, sliced
1 clove garlic, sliced
1 tablespoon oil for frying
4 tomatoes, sliced
1 carrot, sliced
1 stick celery, with leaves, sliced
¼ teaspoon cumin powder
¼ teaspoon chilli powder
¼ teaspoon coriander

Simmer pre-soaked chick peas and lentils in fresh water for
about an hour, until the chick peas are softened. Drain. Fry
onion, garlic, and mince until browned. Transfer to ovenproof
dish. Add chick peas, lentils and remaining ingredients and
reheat to simmering point, stirring to prevent sticking. Bake,
covered, in a pre-heated oven at 180°C for 1 hour. Serve with
brown rice.

Serves 4–6

LAMB AND ONIONS

This dish is simple, but satisfying. The fried onions taste really good with the chops. The butter is needed to enhance the flavour of the fried onions, but can be removed if the dish is prepared in advance. After cooking, cool, then chill in the refrigerator, so that the fat solidifies. Cut the fat off the surface and discard.

8 lamb chops, with fat removed

4 onions, sliced

25–50 g unsalted butter for frying

Fry the onions gently in butter until soft and slightly brown. Transfer to an ovenproof dish. Fry the chops gently until browned on both sides. Drain off as much fat as possible. Transfer chops to the ovenproof dish. Cover and bake at 180°C for 1 hour.

Serves 4

EXOTIC LAMB CHOPS

8 lamb chops, with fat removed

2 onions, sliced

1 clove garlic, sliced

600 g tomatoes, sliced

2 teaspoons rosemary

12 peppercorns

250 ml (1 cup) coconut milk (p. 95)

Simmer onions, garlic, tomatoes, rosemary and peppercorns together for 1 hour. Stir in coconut milk, and reheat gently. Meanwhile grill chops. Pour tomato sauce over chops and serve with rice, noodles or potatoes.

Serves 4

128

LAMB AND TOMATO CASSEROLE

8 lamb chops, with fat removed
1 onion, chopped
2 × 400 g tins unsalted tomatoes
1 tablespoon paprika
6 peppercorns
1 bayleaf
1 teaspoon rosemary
2 tablespoons burghul (cracked wheat)

Place all ingredients in a covered casserole. Bring to simmering point and bake in a pre-heated oven at 180°C for 1 hour.

Serves 4

KIDNEYS AND TOMATO

8 lambs' kidneys
1 onion, sliced
1 carrot, grated
1 capsicum, sliced
1 stick celery, with leaves, sliced
1 clove garlic, sliced
1 tablespoon wholemeal flour
1 teaspoon oregano
½ teaspoon marjoram
black pepper to taste
1 × 400 g tin unsalted tomatoes
½ teaspoon basil

Skin, core and chop kidneys. Simmer all ingredients, except basil, for 1 hour. Add basil and simmer for a few more minutes. Serve with boiled brown rice and a green salad (e.g. bean sprouts, lettuce, cucumber, zucchini and carrot).

Serves 4

Did you know that we recognise most flavours through our sense of smell? Cells scattered throughout the lining of our noses are very sensitive to a wide range of food smells. Even when only tiny amounts of the flavoursome substances evaporate from the food, we can smell them.

Have you ever been enticed into a restaurant by the delicious smell of barbecued chicken, or found yourself unable to resist the temptation of a coffee shop? Have you ever had a heavy cold and found food to be tasteless? If so, you will understand how important our sense of smell is in appreciating flavour.

LIVER AND MUSHROOMS

1 lamb's liver, thinly sliced
1 tablespoon paprika
2 tablespoons wholemeal flour
1 tablespoon olive oil for frying
2 onions, sliced
1 clove garlic, sliced
4 tomatoes, sliced
10–12 mushrooms, sliced
large pinch of basil
2 tablespoons yoghurt
chopped parsley for garnish

Mix paprika and flour together. Coat liver slices with flour mixture. Fry liver until brown. Remove to a dish and keep warm in oven. In the oil used for liver, fry onion, garlic, tomatoes and mushrooms for 5 minutes. Add basil. Cover and simmer for 20 minutes, adding a little water if necessary. Arrange tomato and mushroom sauce around liver on dish. Top liver with yoghurt and sprinkle with parsley.

Serves 4

KIDNEYS AND CORN

8 lambs' kidneys
100 g (2 cups) sweetcorn
water OR stock to cover
80 ml (⅓ cup) yoghurt
1 teaspoon paprika

Skin, core and slice the kidneys. Cover with stock or water. Add paprika. Cover the pan and simmer gently for 1 hour, adding more stock or water if necessary. Add sweetcorn and simmer for 5 minutes. Stir in yoghurt just before serving. Serve with boiled rice or potatoes.

Serves 4

In some parts of Australia the term 'chicken breast' means both sides of the breast. In this book 'chicken breast' means the single, filleted breast.

CHICKEN AND CHOKO CASSEROLE

The mild flavour of the choko is balanced by the spiciness of the tomato sauce in this recipe.

4 chicken breasts, skin and fat removed

6 tomatoes (500 g), sliced

¼ teaspoon sesame oil

1 onion, chopped

1 clove garlic, chopped

1½ cm root ginger, peeled

125 ml (½ cup) water

1 choko, peeled and cubed

6 black peppercorns

1 chilli, seeded and sliced OR ¼ teaspoon chilli powder

1 tablespoon burghul (cracked wheat)

2 tablespoons chopped parsley

125 ml (½ cup) yoghurt

Mix together all ingredients, except yoghurt, and either simmer for 1 hour or bake in pre-heated oven at 180°C for 1 hour. Stir in yoghurt before serving. Fried rice with mushrooms complements this dish well.

Serves 4

CHICKEN AND GREEN VEGETABLES

4 chicken breasts, skin and fat removed, cut into cubes

2 slices root ginger, peeled and finely chopped

1 onion, finely chopped

2 cloves garlic, finely chopped
1/4 teaspoon fenugreek powder
1 tablespoon oil for frying
100 g (2 cups) cauliflower florets
100 g (2 cups) broccoli florets
100 g (2 cups) peas
125 ml (1/2 cup) water
1/3 cup (4 tablespoons) yoghurt

Fry ginger, onion, garlic and fenugreek gently until onion is golden. Add diced chicken and fry lightly. Add vegetables and a little water. Simmer gently for about 20 minutes, until vegetables are tender but still firm. Stir in yoghurt.

Serves 4

CHICKEN AND CORN

This is an attractive dish with the golden corn, the red chilli and the white coconut milk.

4 chicken pieces (e.g. drumsticks, thighs, breasts), skin and fat removed
1 tablespoon oil for frying
1 onion, sliced
100 g (1 cup) corn
1 stick celery, with leaves, sliced
1 chilli, seeded and sliced OR 1/4 teaspoon chilli powder
2 teaspoons paprika
250 ml (1 cup) chicken stock (p. 62)
250 ml (1 cup) coconut milk (p. 95)

Fry chicken until cooked on all sides. Add all other ingredients, except coconut milk, and simmer on top of stove, or in oven at 180°C, for 1 hour. Stir in coconut milk and reheat.

Serves 4

WELSH CHICKEN BREASTS

Mustard and nutmeg form a good combination, in which neither spice dominates. The mustard needs to be dissolved in the milk prior to use so that the enzymes, which produce the spiciness, can work.

4 chicken breasts, skin and fat removed
½ teaspoon mustard powder
2 teaspoons milk
2 teaspoons wholemeal flour
1 teaspoon nutmeg
1 tablespoon oil for coating

Dissolve mustard powder in milk. Mix flour and nutmeg together. Oil breasts on both sides. Grill underside of breasts until browned. Turn and grill outer surface lightly. Baste with milk and mustard mixture, then sprinkle with the flour and nutmeg mixture. Grill until browned and cooked through.

This mixture of spices can also be used to coat a roast chicken.

Serves 4

ASIAN CHICKEN

1 chicken, jointed, with skin and fat removed
1 onion, sliced
1 clove garlic, sliced
1 cm root ginger, peeled and finely chopped
1 tablespoon oil for frying
1 tablespoon curry powder
500 ml (2 cups) water OR *chicken stock (p. 62)*
3 carrots, sliced
2 sticks celery, with leaves, sliced
½ cup broccoli, chopped

1 tomato, sliced

1 small banana, mashed

60 ml (¼ cup) coconut milk (p. 95)

Fry onion, garlic and ginger until soft and golden. Add the curry powder and fry a minute longer. Add the chicken and fry lightly. Cover with stock or water. Add the vegetables and banana. Simmer for about 1 hour, until the chicken is cooked. Stir in the coconut milk and reheat gently. Serve with rice.

Serves 4–5

CHICKEN AND GINGERED VEGETABLES

4 chicken pieces (e.g. drumsticks, thighs), skin and fat removed

1 tablespoon oil for frying

2 cm piece of root ginger, peeled

1 onion, sliced

1 clove garlic, sliced

1 carrot, diced

1 stick celery, with leaves, sliced

50 g (½ cup) corn

1 potato, cubed

50 g (½ cup) peas

500 ml (2 cups) chicken stock (p. 62)

1 tablespoon paprika

white pepper to taste

2 teaspoons lemon grass (optional)

1 tablespoon lemon juice

Fry the chicken pieces until browned. Add the vegetables, cover and fry for a further 5 minutes. Add the stock and spices, and simmer for about 1 hour. Stir in lemon juice.

Serves 4

*T*he flavour of chicken can be varied with herbs and spices. Make gravy the way your grandmother did, from basic ingredients. At all costs avoid gravy mixes. Why? Read their labels!

ROAST CHICKEN WITH HERBS OR SPICES

Many herbs are suitable for sprinkling over a chicken before roasting it (e.g. basil, marjoram, oregano, rosemary, tarragon, thyme). Be cautious with rosemary, tarragon and thyme, all of which have a strong flavour.

Standard times for roasting chicken are calculated as 20 minutes per 500 g, plus 20 minutes extra, at 210°C, in an oven that has been pre-heated.

Spicy roast chicken
1 teaspoon paprika

¼ teaspoon nutmeg

oil

Oil surface of chicken. Rub spices into skin.

Garlic roast chicken
1 clove garlic, chopped

1 teaspoon lemon peel, grated

½ teaspoon savory, chopped

1 teaspoon marjoram

Mix garlic, lemon peel and herbs together. Coat surface of chicken with mixture before roasting.

Rosemary roast chicken
4 small sprigs rosemary

coarse ground black pepper

oil

Oil surface of chicken. Tuck sprigs of rosemary in beside thighs or wings of chicken, or place inside chicken. Sprinkle surface with black pepper.

To make gravy

This is the way to make gravy for all roasts, not just chicken.
* Remove the roast from the roasting pan.
* Gently pour off as much fat as possible, leaving the juices in the pan. (To remove the fat more thoroughly, pour all the fat and juices into a bowl and chill. Save for gravy with your next roast. Cut the solidified fat off the surface and reheat the juices when required.)
* Thicken the juices with wholemeal flour or polenta. Wholemeal flour is nutty; polenta is sweet. Cook the mixture.
* Then use a well-flavoured stock or vegetable water to thin the gravy down to desired consistency. Reheat, stirring constantly, using more stock as gravy thickens. A skinned and chopped tomato can be added and cooked in the gravy to help thicken and flavour it.
* Add a pinch of pepper, paprika or nutmeg to enliven the gravy if necessary. A pinch of herbs, such as marjoram or oregano, may also help.
* Save a little of the juices from a roast as a starter for basting your next roast. This will make the gravy from the next roast much richer!

ROSY CHICKEN

(contributed by Peter Bridgewater)

4 chicken breasts, skin and fat removed

1 tablespoon lemon juice

2 large onions, chopped

25 g unsalted butter

125 ml (½ cup) chicken stock (p. 62)

250 ml (1 cup) sour cream

1 tablespoon paprika

white pepper to taste

1 tablespoon chopped parsley

Sprinkle chicken breasts with lemon juice. Gently fry onions in butter. Add chicken breasts and brown lightly. Bake, covered, in pre-heated oven at 210°C, for 30 minutes. Remove chicken and keep warm on a serving dish. Add stock, cream, paprika and pepper to the remaining juices and boil until the sauce is thick. Pour sauce over chicken breasts and sprinkle with parsley. Serve with rice or boiled new potatoes.

Serves 4

ORIENTAL CHICKEN AND CAPSICUM CASSEROLE

In this recipe I have used sago to thicken the gravy. If you prefer a firmer texture, use burghul or wholemeal flour.

4 chicken pieces (e.g. drumsticks, thighs, breasts), skin and fat removed
1 onion, sliced
1 clove garlic, crushed
1 tablespoon oil for frying
¼ teaspoon sesame oil
250 ml (1 cup) water
375 ml (1½ cups) chicken stock (p. 62)
4 tomatoes, sliced
2 capsicums, sliced
4 tablespoons sago
12 peppercorns
375 ml (1½ cups) coconut milk (p. 95)

Fry chicken, onion and garlic in oils until brown. Add the other ingredients, except coconut milk, and bring to simmering point. Simmer for 1 hour until chicken and vegetables are cooked. Stir in coconut milk and reheat.

Serves 4

CHICKEN STIR-FRY

This is a useful recipe, as it is open to almost infinite variation. Use whatever vegetables are available. Use fresh or cooked chicken, or beef.

200 g (1 cup) chicken meat
1 onion, sliced
1 clove garlic, chopped
1 cm root ginger, peeled and finely chopped
1 tablespoon oil for frying
¼ teaspoon sesame oil
2 teaspoons coriander powder
2 teaspoons cumin powder
¼ teaspoon (or less) chilli powder
¼ teaspoon fenugreek powder
black or white pepper to taste
2–3 carrots, cut into thin sticks
2 sticks celery, with leaves, sliced
8 green beans, sliced
150 g (2 cups) cabbage, shredded
1 tablespoon sherry (optional)
1 tablespoon cornflour
125 ml (½ cup) water

Fry onion, garlic and ginger in the oils, for a few minutes. If using raw chicken meat, add it and cook lightly. Add the spices, carrots, celery and beans and fry gently, turning frequently, until the vegetables are tender. Add water, if necessary. Add the cabbage and chicken, if using cooked meat, and cook again until the cabbage is just tender. Stir in sherry, if desired. Dissolve the cornflour in the 125 ml water and stir in, cooking just until the cornflour is set. Serve with rice. This may be stirred in just before serving.

Serves 4

Avoid frozen chickens, as sodium compounds are added in order to retain moisture. Fresh chickens are preferable. With any chicken, remove the skin and fat to reduce the fat content.

EGG AND CHICKEN CURRY

3 chicken breasts, skin and fat removed, cut into cubes
2 onions, chopped
2 cloves garlic, chopped
1 tablespoon oil for frying
1 cm root ginger, peeled and finely chopped OR 1 teaspoon powdered ginger
1 teaspoon each, turmeric, cumin, paprika
2 teaspoons coriander
2 teaspoons poppyseeds
1 bayleaf
¼ teaspoon chilli powder
black pepper to taste
3 medium-sized carrots, sliced
1 zucchini, sliced
125 ml (½ cup) water
2 hard-boiled eggs, chopped
100 g cabbage, shredded
125 ml (½ cup) yoghurt

Fry onion and garlic until golden. Add diced chicken and fry gently. Add all spices and fry gently for 1–2 minutes. Add carrots and zucchini and a little water. Simmer until vegetables are tender but still firm. Add hard-boiled eggs and cabbage and simmer a further 10 minutes. Add yoghurt and simmer gently for 5 minutes.

Serves 4–6

SALADS WITH A
GREAT FLAVOUR

Essential oils are the components of herbs and spices responsible for their individual flavours. Known chemically as terpenoids, they accumulate in glands on the leaves and in resin ducts elsewhere in the plants. For the best flavour, use young leaves, as the glands dry up as the leaves mature. Cutting, chewing or cooking releases essential oils from the glands and ducts of plants.

EGGPLANT SALAD

1 small eggplant
1 small capsicum
1 small tomato

Dressing

4 tablespoons (⅓ cup) yoghurt
¼ teaspoon marjoram
1 clove garlic, crushed
1 shallot, chopped OR 1 tablespoon onion, chopped
1 tablespoon unsalted tomato paste
white pepper to taste

Bake eggplant, capsicum and tomato, whole, on a baking tray at 190°C for 45 minutes. Remove skin from eggplant and tomato. Cut the eggplant into cubes, the capsicum into thin slices, and mash the tomato. Mix together.

Mix dressing ingredients together. Combine dressing with the vegetables and chill for several hours.

Serves 4

CABBAGE AND SILVER BEET SALAD

75 g (1 cup) shredded cabbage

75 g (1 cup) shredded silver beet

1 tablespoon sunflower seeds for garnish

Dressing

3 tablespoons sour cream OR yoghurt

2 tablespoons water

white pepper to taste

½ teaspoon mustard powder mixed with a little water

Combine cabbage and silver beet. Combine all the dressing ingredients and mix with the vegetables. Sprinkle with sunflower seeds.

Serves 4

COLESLAW

150 g (2 cups) shredded cabbage

2 shallots, thinly sliced

½ cup grated carrot

Dressing

2 tablespoons yoghurt

2 tablespoons lemon juice

¼ teaspoon paprika

¼ teaspoon caraway seeds

Combine cabbage, shallots and carrot. Mix dressing ingredients together and stir into vegetables.

Serves 4

Commercially prepared salad dressings, mayonnaise, pickled onions, chutneys, etc., all contain added salt. Prepare your own salad dressings. They can then be low in fat and kilojoules as well as low in salt. Dressings will keep for some time in the refrigerator. Some chopped herbs scattered through a salad can be enough to add interesting flavour.

CUCUMBER AND PARSLEY SALAD

1 cucumber, peeled

Dressing
2 tablespoons yoghurt OR sour cream

2 tablespoons parsley, chopped

1 teaspoon lovage, chopped (optional)

white pepper to taste

Grate the cucumber. Mix the dressing ingredients together. Mix the dressing with the cucumber.

Serves 4

CUCUMBER, MINT AND YOGHURT SALAD

1 cucumber, peeled or unpeeled, as desired

Dressing
4 tablespoons (⅓ cup) yoghurt

1 tablespoon mint, chopped

1 clove garlic, crushed

1 teaspoon lemon balm, chopped (optional)

Chop or slice cucumber. Mix dressing ingredients together and add to cucumber.

Serves 4–6

TOMATO SALAD

4 large tomatoes, sliced

Dressing
4 tablespoons lemon juice

2 tablespoons unsalted tomato paste

4 tablespoons water

1 tablespoon onion, thinly sliced and finely chopped

1 teaspoon fresh basil, chopped OR a pinch of dried basil

black pepper to taste

Place tomatoes in serving dish. Mix all dressing ingredients together and pour over tomato. Chill and serve.

Serves 4

*S*alt is not essential for keeping cool in hot conditions or after physical exertion, provided your normal diet is low in sodium. People on a low-sodium diet produce sweat low in sodium. The concentration of sodium does not change suddenly when sweat flow increases, and so the body is not depleted of sodium. People living on a high-sodium diet produce sweat with a high concentration of sodium. When they sweat, their bodies continue to pump out sodium at a high concentration and so their bodies are more rapidly depleted.

CAPSICUM AND CUCUMBER SALAD

1 cucumber, thinly sliced (and peeled if desired)
1 capsicum, thinly sliced
2 teaspoons fresh dill, chopped

Alternate a layer of cucumber with a layer of capsicum in a bowl, sprinkling the dill between each layer.

Serves 4

CARROT AND GREEN BEAN SALAD

2 cups green beans, sliced
2 small carrots, grated

Dressing
1 tablespoon lemon juice
2 tablespoons oil
pinch of thyme

Mix dressing ingredients together. Add to vegetables and chill.

Serves 4

FLORET SALAD

100 g (1 cup) cauliflower florets

100 g (1 cup) broccoli florets

Dressing
250 ml (1 cup) yoghurt

¼ teaspoon fenugreek powder

pinch of turmeric

Prepare this salad in advance, as this allows time for the flavours to develop fully, and for the dressing to become a delicate pale yellow colour.

Cut the florets into very small pieces. Mix the dressing ingredients together. Combine florets and yoghurt dressing.

Serves 4

BEANS AND CELERY SALAD

1 cup green beans, sliced

1 stick celery, sliced

Dressing
2 tablespoons yoghurt

¼ teaspoon mint, chopped

pepper to taste

Mix all ingredients together.

Serves 2–3

Variation
Use sliced carrots instead of beans.

SMOOTH AND CRUNCHY SALAD

1 carrot, diced

1 stick celery, with leaves, sliced

Dressing
250 ml (1 cup) yoghurt

½ teaspoon mint, finely chopped

½ teaspoon salad burnet, finely chopped (optional)

Mix all ingredients together and chill before serving. Serve as a contrast to any spicy dish.

Serves 2–4

NIBBLES

*T*asty, unsalted dips or salt-free nibbles are quite delightful before a meal. Fresh unsalted cottage cheese is available from gourmet shops, and it forms an excellent basis for dips. Unsalted nuts are readily available.

Remember
- Packet dips depend to a large extent on salt and other sodium compounds for their 'taste'.
- Even cream cheese and ordinary cottage cheese, which taste fairly bland, contain added salt.
- Savoury cheese snacks contain not only added salt, but also cheese, itself a salty ingredient.
- Most savoury biscuits are very salty and thus unsuitable to serve with dips. Instead, serve fresh vegetable pieces or fingers of toasted, unsalted bread.

BASIC DIP

100 g unsalted cottage cheese

3 tablespoons yoghurt

Mix cheese and yoghurt together and add flavouring as required. (See following suggestions.)

AVOCADO DIP

1 ripe avocado

100 g unsalted cottage cheese

2 tablespoons yoghurt

4 thin slices of onion, finely chopped

2 teaspoons chopped parsley

Mash or blend avocado, cheese and yoghurt together until smooth. Add onion and parsley and refrigerate for at least 1 hour to allow flavours to develop.

CHEESE DIP

100 g unsalted cottage cheese

3 tablespoons yoghurt

25 g low-sodium cheese

Mix the cottage cheese and yoghurt. Melt the low-sodium cheese in a pan and remove from heat. Immediately add some of the yoghurt and cottage cheese mixture. Gradually add the rest of the mixture and stir until smooth. Refrigerate for at least 1 hour, to allow flavours to develop.

TOMATO DIP

100 g unsalted cottage cheese

3 tablespoons yoghurt

1 tablespoon unsalted tomato paste

½ teaspoon paprika

pinch of chilli powder (optional)

4 thin slices onion, finely chopped

1 teaspoon lemon juice (optional)

Purée, or mix together, all ingredients except lemon juice. Test the flavour and, if necessary, enhance with lemon juice. Refrigerate for at least 1 hour, to allow flavours to develop.

PRAWN DIP

12–15 small green prawns
100 g unsalted cottage cheese
3 tablespoon yoghurt
½ teaspoon fresh dill, chopped
1 teaspoon lemon juice (optional)

Cook the prawns by dropping them into boiling water and simmering for 3 minutes. Remove shells. Purée prawns with cheese, yoghurt and dill. Test the flavour and, if necessary, enhance with lemon juice. Refrigerate for at least 1 hour, to allow flavours to develop.

HUMUS

Humus is becoming increasingly popular, as a dip or as an accompaniment for meat dishes, such as kebabs. Here is my unsalted version of it.

100 g (½ cup) chick peas, soaked overnight, drained and cooked in fresh water until soft
4 tablespoons lemon juice
2 cloves garlic
3 tablespoons tahini
paprika and chopped parsley for garnish

Drain the chick peas and purée with the lemon juice and garlic. If the paste is too stiff, add a little water. Slowly add the tahini, and purée further until ingredients are well blended and the paste is smooth. Test the flavour and add more lemon juice if necessary. Add the garnish.

FALAFEL

250 g (1⅓ cups) chick peas, soaked overnight, drained and cooked in fresh water until soft

250 g (1 cup) yellow split peas, soaked overnight, drained and cooked in fresh water until soft

2 teaspoons cumin powder

2 teaspoons coriander powder

¼ teaspoon chilli powder

wholemeal flour for coating

oil for deep frying

Mix drained chick peas and split peas. Add the spices. Mince the mixture and form into flat cakes (a rounded dessertspoonful will make one cake). Coat with flour and deep fry until golden brown.

Makes 12–20 cakes

Variation
Substitute the following for the spices above:

1 shallot, chopped

1 onion, chopped

1 clove garlic, chopped

1 tablespoon oil for frying

1 teaspoon cumin powder

2 teaspoons coriander powder

2 teaspoons fenugreek powder

2 teaspoons paprika

¼ teaspoon chilli powder

Fry the shallot, onion and garlic gently before adding them, with the spices, to the chick peas and split peas.

CHICK PEA NIBBLES

125 g (½ cup) chick peas, soaked overnight, drained and cooked in fresh water until soft

1 tablespoon wholemeal flour

1 teaspoon paprika

pinch of chilli powder (for 'hot' chick peas use ¼ teaspoon chilli powder)

1 beaten egg

1–2 tablespoons oil for frying

Mix flour, paprika and chilli powder. Roll drained chick peas in egg, then coat with flour mixture. Shallow-fry coated chick peas until flour is browned. Serve as savoury nibbles.

These are best served immediately, while still hot, but they can be prepared in advance and served cold.

Makes approximately 150

TASTY TOAST FINGERS

1 clove of garlic OR ½ teaspoon of ONE of the following: paprika, curry powder, prepared mustard

25 g unsalted butter OR margarine

6–7 slices unsalted bread

2–3 tablespoons sesame seeds

Crush the garlic, or mix the spice, into the butter or margarine.

EITHER spread the bread with the desired mixture, cut it into fingers, sprinkle liberally with sesame seeds, and bake in a pre-heated oven at 220°C for 20 minutes;

OR toast one side of the bread, turn over and spread with butter mixture, cut it into fingers, and sprinkle with sesame seeds, then grill until the sesame seeds are toasted.

Beware all small-goods, such as sausages, salami, ham, wursts, pâté. Once you are used to an unsalted diet, you will realise that the taste of most of these is due to the large amount of salt they contain. Frankfurters on sticks, pâtés on biscuits, smoked oysters, etc., should be avoided at parties (and any other time).

FRIED AVOCADO

1 avocado

1 tablespoon wholemeal flour

2 teaspoons paprika

1–2 tablespoons oil for frying

Peel and remove stone from avocado. Slice avocado flesh. Mix flour and paprika. Coat avocado slices in flour and paprika mixture. Fry avocado slices until browned.

Serve with pre-dinner drinks or as a vegetable with baked fish, roast or grilled meat.

CHEESE BALLS

2 tablespoons finely chopped celery

2 tablespoons finely chopped onion

2 teaspoons oil OR unsalted butter for frying

50 g (4 tablespoons) unsalted cottage cheese

2 tablespoons poppyseeds

1 tablespoon coarsely ground black pepper

Fry the celery and onion gently until soft. Drain off as much oil as possible. Mix the celery and onion into the cheese. Roll the cheese mixture into balls about the size of hazelnuts. Roll them in the poppyseeds and pepper.

Makes 14 balls

CHICKEN LIVER PÂTÉ

1 medium onion, finely chopped

1 clove garlic, finely chopped

50 g unsalted butter

250 g chicken livers

pinch of thyme and marjoram

1 bayleaf

black pepper to taste

2–3 tablespoons white wine

chives and parsley for garnish

Fry onion and garlic gently in butter. Add the chicken livers. Add the herbs, wrapped in muslin (bouquet garni), and pepper. Fry until the livers are cooked, but still soft. Stir in the wine and cook a minute longer. Remove herbs. Puree the liver mixture stirring in more wine if necessary. Place mixture in a small pot, and refrigerate. Garnish with chopped chives and parsley. Serve with toast fingers made from unsalted bread.

POTATO STRAWS

100 g cold mashed potato

100 g (²⁄₃ cup) wholemeal flour

50 g low-sodium cheese, grated

2 tablespoons water

1 egg, beaten, for glazing

sesame seeds

Mix potato, flour and cheese until well blended. Stir in water to form a stiff pastry. Roll out on a floured board and cut into strips or rounds. Place on a greased baking tray and brush with beaten egg. Sprinkle with sesame seeds. Bake at 200°C for 15–20 minutes until brown on top. Eat immediately.

156

BREADS AND
BUNS

Tips on bread making

- *Rye flour takes longer to rise than wholemeal or other flours.*
- *Rye flour gives flavour.*
- *For a dark wholemeal bread, use 1:1 wholemeal: plain flour.*
- *For a light wholemeal bread, use 1:2 wholemeal: plain flour.*
- *Potato makes the bread lighter.*
- *Sugar, molasses or honey can be used to activate the yeast.*
- *Potato allows the yeast to act, without the addition of sugar.*
- *Oil can be used if desired. Do not use olive oil as this has too strong a flavour.*
- *Seeds can be added either with the yeast or when kneading the dough.*
- *Garlic or onion can be added with the yeast. Crush the garlic really well. Grate the onion finely.*
- *To punch down the dough: remove it from the bowl when it has doubled in size, punch it with balled fists (not too hard) once or twice, then shape as required.*

EASY BREAD

(contributed by Kari Stunden)

25 g (3 tablespoons) dried yeast OR 50 g compressed yeast

750 ml (3 cups) warm water

1 small potato

750 g (5 cups) plain flour, preferably stoneground

250 g (1⅔ cups) rye flour

500 g (3⅓ cups) stoneground wholemeal flour

Dissolve yeast in water. Grate potato into water and yeast mixture and leave for a few minutes until the mixture starts to foam. Mix flours together, then stir in yeast mixture. Combine thoroughly.

Knead the dough on a floured board for a few minutes. When the dough is soft and pliable, place it in an oiled bowl and slide it around until the surface is covered in oil. This prevents a hard crust forming as the dough rises. Cover with a cloth, and leave in a warm place to rise (about 30 minutes), until it has doubled in bulk.

Pre-heat oven to 210°C. Tip dough onto a floured board and knead lightly. Shape into loaves. Roll in oatmeal, if desired. Bake for 30 minutes. Place on a rack to cool.

Makes 3 loaves

Variation

For a fruit loaf, use 1:1 water:milk; add an egg and a knob of unsalted butter; add 2 cups peel/dried fruit rolled in sugar. Glaze with egg and sprinkle with sugar.

BARA BRITH

Bara brith is a Welsh fruit loaf. I have adapted this recipe to make it free of added sodium.

125 ml (½ cup) milk
125 ml (½ cup) water
1 tablespoon black treacle
1 egg, beaten
15 g (2 tablespoons) dried yeast OR 25 g compressed yeast
300 g (2 cups) plain flour
300 g (2 cups) wholemeal flour
1 teaspoon mixed spice
2 tablespoons chopped peel
200 g (1½ cups) mixed dried fruit (currants, raisins, sultanas)
honey OR egg for glazing

Warm milk, water and treacle slightly. Cool to lukewarm. Add the beaten egg. Crumble yeast into the lukewarm mixture and leave for a few minutes until it starts to foam. Mix together flours, spices and fruit. Stir in milk and yeast mixture.

Knead the dough on a floured board for a few minutes until it is pliable. Place the dough in an oiled bowl and slide it around until the surface is covered in oil. This prevents a dry crust forming while the dough is rising. Cover with a clean cloth and leave in a warm place to rise (about 30 minutes).

Pre-heat oven to 220°C. Punch dough down, form into a loaf shape and put in a greased loaf tin (22 × 9 × 9 cm). Leave to rise in a warm place for 15 minutes. Glaze with honey or egg and bake for 20 minutes. Reduce oven to 170°C and bake a further 45 minutes. Turn onto a rack to air.

ARABIAN ENVELOPES

1½ tablespoons sesame seeds
1 teaspoon cumin seeds

1 teaspoon poppyseeds

1 teaspoon aniseed

pinch of ginger

125 ml (½ cup) water

7 g (1 tablespoon) dried yeast OR 12–15 g compressed yeast

1 teaspoon raw sugar

150 g (1 cup) plain flour

100 g (⅔ cup) wholemeal flour

1 egg, beaten OR milk for glaze

Filling

200 g (1 cup) unsalted ricotta cheese

1–2 tablespoons onion, finely chopped or grated

black pepper to taste

Mix together the sesame and cumin seeds. Roast or toast them lightly. Combine with other spices.

Warm water to lukewarm. Crumble yeast into sugar and leave for a few minutes until mixture starts to foam. Stir in warm water. Combine flours and 2 tablespoons of the seed mix. Stir yeast mixture into flour. Mix thoroughly.

Knead the dough on a floured board for a few minutes. When it is soft and pliable, place it in an oiled bowl and slide it around until the surface is covered in oil. This prevents a hard crust forming as the dough rises. Cover with a cloth, and leave in a warm place to rise (about 30 minutes).

Prepare filling by mixing all filling ingredients together. Pre-heat oven to 220°C. Turn the dough onto a floured board and cut into six pieces. Roll out each piece into a square. Place some filling mixture in the centre of each piece, and fold the corners of the dough over to make a sealed envelope.

Place envelopes on a greased baking sheet and brush with beaten egg or milk. Sprinkle with the remainder of the seed mix. Leave in a warm place to rise (about 15 minutes). Bake for 15–20 minutes.

Makes 6 envelopes

HERBAL CHEESE BREADS

125 ml (½ cup) yoghurt
7 g (1 tablespoon) dried yeast OR 12–15 g compressed yeast
1 teaspoon raw sugar
150 g (1 cup) plain flour
100 g (⅔ cup) wholemeal flour
1 teaspoon paprika
1 teaspoon basil
1 teaspoon marjoram
1 teaspoon thyme
1–2 tablespoons fresh chives OR onion, finely chopped
1 clove garlic, finely chopped
1 egg, beaten OR milk for glaze
poppyseeds

Filling

200 g (1 cup) unsalted cottage cheese
1–2 tablespoons fresh parsley, chopped
white pepper to taste

Warm yoghurt slightly (if overheated, it will curdle). Crumble yeast into sugar and leave for a few minutes until mixture starts to foam. Combine yeast and yoghurt. Mix together flours, paprika, herbs and garlic. Stir yeast mixture into flour mixture and combine thoroughly. Add water if necessary.

Knead the dough on a floured board for a few minutes. When it is soft and pliable, place it in an oiled bowl and slide it around until the surface is covered in oil. This prevents a hard crust forming as the dough rises. Cover with a cloth, and leave in a warm place to rise (about 30 minutes).

Prepare filling by mixing all filling ingredients together. Preheat oven to 220°C. Turn dough onto a floured board and divide into 6 pieces. Roll out each piece into a square. Place some filling in the middle of each piece and fold over corners of dough to form a sealed envelope.

Place envelopes on a greased baking sheet and brush with beaten egg or milk. Sprinkle with poppyseeds, if desired. Leave to rise, in a warm place (about 15 minutes). Bake for 15–20 minutes.

Makes 6 envelopes

NATURAL ROLLS

Yeast requires sugar to start the fermentation process, which is used to leaven bread. Many fruits and vegetables contain sugars, and can be used instead of pure sugar as your yeast starter. Grating (or mashing) opens up the fruit or vegetable, releasing some of its sugars. More sugars are released during simmering, as this breaks open the cells, allowing the sugars to flow out.

1 small carrot, finely grated

2–3 tablespoons + ⅓ cup water

7 g (1 tablespoon) dried yeast OR 12–15 g compressed yeast

150 g (1 cup) plain flour

100 g (⅔ cup) wholemeal flour

milk OR beaten egg for glazing

poppyseeds OR sesame seeds for decoration (optional)

Simmer carrot in 2–3 tablespoons water for about 3 minutes. Cool to lukewarm. (The carrot can be used raw, but the yeast will take longer to act.) Crumble yeast into carrot, and leave for a few minutes until the mixture starts to rise. Mix ⅓ cup water into carrot and yeast mixture, and stir into flours. Combine thoroughly.

Knead the dough on a floured board for a few minutes. When the dough is soft and pliable, place it in an oiled bowl and slide it around until the surface is covered in oil, then cover bowl with a dry cloth or place it in a margarine or ice-cream container with a lid. Covering will prevent the dough forming a hard crust as it rises. Leave in a warm place to rise (about 30 minutes), until it has doubled in bulk.

Pre-heat oven to 220°C. Punch down and divide dough into 6 pieces. Shape each piece into a roll. Place on an oiled baking tray. Leave to rise in a warm place for about 15 minutes. Glaze with milk or beaten egg, and sprinkle with poppy-seeds or sesame seeds, if desired. Bake for 15–20 minutes.

Makes 6 rolls

CARAWAY ROLLS

Using the recipe for Natural Rolls (p. 163), add ¼ teaspoon caraway seeds to the flours before stirring in the carrot mixture. This quantity of caraway seeds is enough to add a pleasant flavour to the rolls, without being too strong. If caraway really appeals to you, add more.

*F*resh rolls are always appetising. They need no salt and are quite delicious when served straight from the oven. (If you can't serve the bread immediately, warm it up slightly before serving.) Fancy shapes, glazing and sprinkling with seeds also make rolls more interesting. Baking bread in a ceramic flower pot (the common or garden kind — unused for plants, but washed and greased like a baking tin) works well and brings interesting comments.

TOMATO ROLLS

1 tablespoon unsalted tomato paste OR *1 tomato*
1–2 tablespoons water (if using tomato paste)
7 g (1 tablespoon) dried yeast OR *12–15 g compressed yeast*
100 g (²⁄₃ cup) wholemeal flour
150 g (1 cup) plain flour
¹⁄₂ teaspoon cumin powder
¹⁄₂ teaspoon coriander powder
125 ml (¹⁄₂ cup) additional water

Mix tomato paste and 1–2 tablespoons of water together, or slice and simmer tomato until soft. Remove skin. Crumble yeast into tomato mixture and leave for a few minutes until the mixture starts to rise. Combine flours and cumin and coriander. Mix tomato and yeast mixture and 125 ml (½ cup) water into the flours.

Knead the dough on a floured board for a few minutes. When the dough is soft and pliable, place it in an oiled bowl and slide it around until the surface is covered in oil, then cover bowl with a dry cloth or place it in a margarine or ice-cream container with a lid. Leave in a warm place to rise (about 30 minutes), until it has doubled in bulk.

Pre-heat oven to 220°C. Punch down and divide dough into 6 pieces. Shape each piece into a roll. Place on an oiled baking tray. Leave to rise, in a warm place (about 15 minutes). Bake for 15–20 minutes.

165

Ordinary breads and buns are heavily salted, and can contribute considerably to your sodium intake. Make your own bread or find a baker who makes salt-free or salt-reduced breads.

ZUCCHINI ROLLS

1 small zucchini, cooked and mashed
7 g (1 tablespoon) dried yeast OR 12–15 g compressed yeast
100 g (²⁄₃ cup) wholemeal flour
150 g (1 cup) plain flour
1 teaspoon chopped mint
125 ml (¹⁄₂ cup) water

Crumble yeast into mashed zucchini and leave for a few minutes until the mixture starts to rise. Combine flours and mint. Mix zucchini and yeast mixture and the water into the flours.

Knead the dough on a floured board for a few minutes. When the dough is soft and pliable, place it in an oiled bowl and slide it around until the surface is covered in oil, then cover bowl with a dry cloth or place it in a margarine or ice-cream container with a lid. Leave in a warm place to rise (about 30 minutes), until it has doubled in bulk.

Pre-heat oven to 220°C. Punch down and divide dough into 6 pieces. Shape each piece into a roll. Place on an oiled baking tray. Leave to rise, in a warm place (about 15 minutes). Bake for 15–20 minutes.

SPICED OR HOT CROSS BUNS

These buns are appetising at any time of year, but can be made specially for Easter by putting a cross on the top.

125 ml (¹⁄₂ cup) milk

200 g (½ cup) each sultanas, currants and mixed peel OR
200 g (1½ cups) dried fruit of choice

30 g salt-free margarine OR *3 tablespoons (¼ cup) oil*

1 egg, beaten

15 g (2 tablespoons) dried yeast OR *25 g compressed yeast*

125 ml (½ cup) warm water

150 g (1 cup) plain flour

450 g (3 cups) wholemeal flour

1½ teaspoons mixed spice

Cross mixture

2½ tablespoons of plain flour

2 tablespoons water

Warm milk, dried fruit and margarine or oil slightly. Cool to lukewarm. Add beaten egg. Dissolve yeast in warm water. Add cooled milk and egg mixture and leave for a few minutes until it starts to foam. Mix together flour and spice. Stir milk and yeast mixture into dry mixture and combine thoroughly.

Knead the dough on a floured board for about 10 minutes, adding more wholemeal flour if dough is too sticky. When the dough is smooth and elastic, place it in an oiled bowl and slide it around until the surface is covered in oil. This prevents a hard crust forming as the dough rises. Cover with a clean cloth and leave in a warm place to rise (about 30 minutes).

Pre-heat oven to 200°C. Separate dough into about 16 pieces and form into buns. Place on a greased, floured baking dish and leave to rise in a warm place (about 15 minutes).

To make crosses, mix cross dough, roll out and cut into strips. Moisten surface of buns with water, milk or beaten egg and place strips in form of a cross on top. Bake for about 20 minutes.

Makes 16 buns

CAKES AND OTHER DESSERTS

It is easy to cut out salt from cakes and desserts, as the salt makes little difference to the flavour. Try your favourite recipes without salt and you will see what I mean. For recipes that require sodium bicarbonate or baking powder, substitute a potassium-based baking powder (see below).

Flavourings for desserts include the results of browning, as in the baking of cakes; the flavours of fruits, each of which has an individual flavour; and the flavours of herbs, spices and essences.

- *Some mints — such as apple mint and peppermint, lemon balm, or even lemon thyme — can add a touch of flavour to summer desserts, but be careful as their flavours can be quite strong.*
- *Aniseed, cardamom, cinnamon, cloves, ginger, mace and nutmeg are all sweet spices that can be used as dessert flavourings. Take care, especially with the less familiar flavours, as these spices are quite pervasive. Orange-blossom water and rose water (obtainable from pharmacists), as well as the more familiar vanilla essence, also are useful for flavouring desserts.*

POTASSIUM-BASED BAKING POWDER

(contributed by Dr Trevor Beard)

Ask your pharmacist to prepare sodium-free, potassium-based baking powder according to this recipe. As there is a dispensing fee, some people have a kilogram made up at a time, but you can certainly ask for a smaller quantity.

potassium bitartrate (cream of tartar)	*428 g*
potassium bicarbonate	*303 g*
maize cornflour (prevents caking)	*212 g*

tartaric acid	*57 g*
TOTAL WEIGHT	*1000 g*

A recipe that would use one teaspoonful of ordinary baking powder will need about 1½ teaspoons of sodium-free baking powder. The amount needed depends on the presence and quantity of other ingredients, such as egg, but in general you will need to use about 1½–3 level teaspoons of this powder to 150 g (1 cup) of wholemeal flour. With some white flours you can manage with a little less.

Remember that some foods and drugs interact. If you are on medication for high blood pressure or advanced kidney failure, ask your doctor whether extra potassium is permitted.

CARROT CAKE

Such a favourite as carrot cake has many variations. Here is my basic, unsalted recipe for you to vary as you wish.

100 g (½ cup) raw sugar
3 eggs
200 ml (¾ cup) oil
3 teaspoons potassium-based baking powder (p. 170)
300 g (2 cups) wholemeal flour
1¼ teaspoons cinnamon
1 teaspoon vanilla essence
2 cups finely grated carrot

Beat sugar and eggs together until frothy. Add oil and mix. Stir in baking powder, flour, cinnamon and vanilla. Fold in grated carrot. Pour into greased, round 20 cm baking tin. Bake in pre-heated oven at 180°C for from 1½ to 2 hours.

This cake can also be served as a dessert with fresh yoghurt and topped with chopped nuts.

Serves 10–12

*R*emember *that both bicarbonate of soda and ordinary baking powder contain sodium. As a raising agent use either yeast, or a potassium-based baking powder. Potassium-based baking powder and potassium bicarbonate made under the proprietary name Salt Skip are available in the major cities of Australia, as are Salt Skip wholemeal potassium-based self-raising flour and unbleached white potassium-based self-raising flour. If you have difficulty in locating these products, please write to the author, who will put you in touch with the distributor.*

WHOLEMEAL APPLE AND SULTANA CAKE

Cake mixture

50 g salt-free margarine

50 g (4 tablespoons) brown sugar

1 egg

80 ml (4 tablespoons) milk

150 g (1 cup) Salt Skip wholemeal self-raising flour OR 150 g wholemeal flour plus 3 teaspoons potassium-based baking powder (p. 170)

25 g (2 tablespoons) sultanas

Topping

½ teaspoon cinnamon

1 tablespoon brown sugar

1 apple, peeled and sliced

Mix all cake mixture ingredients, except sultanas, together in mixer. Stir in sultanas. Put mixture into greased, round 18 cm baking tin and spread evenly. Mix brown sugar and cinnamon together. Decorate top of cake with sliced apple and sprinkle with cinnamon and sugar mixture. Bake in pre-heated oven at 180°C for 45 minutes.

Serves 8–10

FLAPJACKS

Easy and quick to prepare, these flapjacks were a favourite recipe of my mother. They are still a favourite dish with children today, but are not for people on low-fat diets.

150 g unsalted butter
⅔ cup (150 g) raw sugar
1⅔ cups (200 g) rolled oats

Warm butter and sugar together, stirring until sugar is dissolved. Stir in oats. Lay mixture on baking tray and press down firmly. Bake in pre-heated oven at 180°C for 20 minutes. Score the surface to form fingers while still hot. Leave to cool, then turn out.

Makes 16

ANISEED BALLS

300 g (2 cups) wholemeal flour
3 tablespoons oil
125 ml (½ cup) water
⅓ cup (4 tablespoons) aniseed
100 g (½ cup) raw sugar
50 g (½ cup) sesame seeds

Mix flour and oil together. Gradually add water until the dough is soft but firm. Add aniseed and knead the dough. Add the sugar and knead again. Form into small balls, about the size of a nut. Roll balls in sesame seeds and place on a greased baking tray. Bake in pre-heated oven at 180°C for from 45 minutes to 1 hour.

Makes 16–20

Remember that sodium bicarbonate is a compound that introduces extra sodium into your diet. So beware of cake mixes or bought cakes and prepared cake or pastry-style desserts. These will almost certainly contain sodium bicarbonate, and usually salt as well.

SURPRISE CAKE

I call this Surprise Cake because most people are surprised to learn that one of the main ingredients is a very humble vegetable.

4 tablespoons sugar
2 eggs
125 ml (½ cup) oil
2 teaspoons potassium-based baking powder (p. 170)
2 teaspoons ginger
200 g (1⅓ cups) wholemeal flour
2 tablespoons raisins
2 tablespoons currants
150 g (1¼ cups) finely grated turnip
sesame seeds for decoration

Mix all ingredients, except sesame seeds, raisins, currants and turnip, together in mixer for 3 minutes. Fold in raisins, currants and grated turnip. Pour into a greased rectangular cake tin (19 × 9 cm and 6 cm deep). Sprinkle on sesame seeds. Bake in pre-heated oven at 180°C for 1 hour.

Serves 6–8

You will find that as your palate adjusts to a lesser amount of salt in your diet, you will become more sensitive to sweetness. You may find that at first you need to add more sugar to recipes than I have recommended, but eventually you may even want to omit sugar altogether.

SWEDISH APPLE CAKE

This recipe is based on a Swedish Apple Cake recipe that is absolutely delicious. It has the advantage that it can be prepared in advance and reheated just before serving.

100 g (1 cup) burghul (cracked wheat), soaked overnight and drained

400 g apples, cored, peeled and sliced

water for simmering apples

raw sugar to taste (about 2 tablespoons)

50 g unsalted butter

Soak the burghul for several hours (overnight, if possible). Simmer the apples and half the sugar in a very little water, until the apples are soft (10–15 minutes). Mash the apples to form a purée. Gently fry the softened burghul in butter and remainder of the sugar. Place layers of apple purée and burghul mixture alternately in a 1½ litre, greased baking dish. Finish with a layer of burghul mixture. Warm the mixture through in a pre-heated oven at 150°C for 30 minutes. Serve with yoghurt, if desired.

Serves 4–6

PLUM PIZZA

This recipe is surprisingly easy, although the instructions appear long.

Dough
2 teaspoons dried yeast

1 tablespoon plum juice (from the stewed plums)

3 tablespoons water

75 g (½ cup) plain flour

50 g (⅓ cup) wholemeal flour

½ teaspoon cinnamon

Filling
300 g plums, stewed or tinned, stone removed and chopped

sugar to taste (unnecessary with tinned plums)

1 tablespoon wheatgerm

Mix the yeast with a little plum juice. Stand for a few minutes until the mixture starts to froth. Add water. Combine flours and cinnamon and stir in yeast mixture. Mix dough thoroughly, and then knead until soft and pliable (about 10 minutes). Place dough, covered with a clean cloth, in a warm place for about 30 minutes, or until the dough has doubled in size.

Pre-heat the oven to 210°C. Grease a pie dish (19 cm diameter). Punch down the dough and roll it into a circle. Line the bottom of the pie dish with the dough. Stand for about 15 minutes in a warm place, until the dough has risen. Bake for 20 minutes.

Remove from oven and spread the stewed plums over the surface. Sprinkle with wheatgerm. Bake for a further 5 minutes.

If not serving immediately, turn the pizza onto a rack to air.

Serves 4–6

Variation
Use 300 g stewed apples, 1–2 tablespoons sultanas and ½ teaspoon cinnamon for filling instead of plums.

APPLES AND SAGO

The use of sago with stewed apples makes an old recipe a little bit different.

3 tablespoons sago

sugar to taste (about 1 tablespoon)

500 ml (2 cups) water

400 g apples, peeled, cored and sliced

1 tablespoon lemon juice

Simmer sago and sugar in the water until the sago is clear (about 15 minutes). Add the apples and lemon juice and simmer for a further 15 minutes, until the apples are tender.

Serves 4

BAKED BANANA

This dessert is quite rich, so I recommend small servings.

2 small bananas

250 ml (1 cup) yoghurt

1/4 teaspoon cardamom

Blend all ingredients together until thoroughly mixed. Pour into a greased ovenproof dish. Bake at 180°C for 20 minutes. The mixture should still be runny, rather like custard. If baked for too long it becomes cheesey.

Serves 3–4

The best dessert of all is fresh fruit. Fresh fruit needs no cooking and creates little or no washing up! Fresh fruit provides endless variety — try some of the exotic fruits, relatively new to the Australian market, such as babaco, pepino or kiwano. Fresh fruit provides a range of flavours, without added sugar, fat or salt. In these health-conscious days, what more could you want?

ROSE PEARS

4–5 pears
120 ml (½ cup) water
1 teaspoon rose water
1 tablespoon raw sugar

Peel, core and quarter pears. Add other ingredients to pears. Simmer gently until pears are tender (about 15 minutes). Serve with yoghurt, if desired.

Serves 4

GRAPEFRUIT AND GINGER DELIGHT

This is a rich dessert, which is both tart and sweet.

1 grapefruit
2 avocados
raw sugar to taste (about 2 teaspoons)
4 tablespoons yoghurt
1–1½ teaspoons ginger
a pinch of cinnamon
50 g ginger in syrup, chopped

Remove flesh from grapefruit and purée it in the blender. Remove flesh from the avocado and mash it. Keep the avocado shells for serving. Purée the grapefruit, mashed avocado, sugar and yoghurt until the mixture is fairly fluffy. Add the spices a little at a time, testing the flavour after each addition. Stir in the chopped ginger and spoon mixture into the avocado shells or bowls. Serve chilled.

Serves 4–6

EASY FRUIT SAUCE

This makes an excellent sauce for ice-cream (be careful that the ice-cream you buy does not contain added salt). Or it can be served as a dessert in its own right.

2 small apples

2 oranges

12 chopped nuts (any type of nut will do, but macadamias are preferred)

Peel, core and slice the apples. Peel and segment or chop the oranges. Purée the apples and oranges together until the mixture has a fluffy texture. Chill. Sprinkle with nuts before serving.

Serves 4

Variation

1 × 440 g tin pineapple

2 tablespoons pineapple juice

2 small apples

Prepare as above.

Vary your fruit desserts by simply puréeing fruit, puréeing and freezing it, making a sorbet, baking it, stewing it, chopping it, chopping and mixing it (fruit salad), serving it in the hollowed out shells of fruit (e.g. pineapple, orange, grapefruit or melon), serving it with yoghurt or decorating it with herbs. Tinned fruits can also be used to add to the variety of fruit.

BUDERIM ORANGES

juice of 2 oranges
1 teaspoon honey
4 oranges, peeled and segmented
50 g crystallised ginger, finely chopped
½ teaspoon nutmeg

Pour orange juice into a serving bowl. Dissolve honey in it. Chop the orange segments. Stir the oranges, ginger and nutmeg into the orange juice until all ingredients are thoroughly mixed. Chill.

Serves 4

ORANGE AND MANGO WATER ICE

juice of 5 oranges
1 × 170 g tin mango pulp

Mix the orange juice and mango pulp together. Pour the mixture into a freezerproof container. Freeze for an hour or two. As the mixture freezes, stir it with a fork to break up the ice crystals a few times, so that the final ice is light and crunchy and not a solid block.

Serves 4

PEACH AND PASSIONFRUIT SORBET

1 × 425 g tin peaches in natural juice

1 × 170 g tin passionfruit in syrup

1 egg white

Drain the peaches and save the juice. Purée the peaches, adding enough juice to make the purée moist (1–2 tablespoons). Discard the remainder of the juice. Stir in the passionfruit pulp. Pour mixture into a freezerproof container and freeze until mushy (1–2 hours). Beat the egg white until stiff and fold into the frozen mixture. Return to freezer and freeze until solid.

Serves 4–6

Variation

For an even simpler sorbet, use the tin of passionfruit with a tablespoon of lemon juice. Just mix together, freeze until mushy, stir in the beaten egg white and freeze until solid.

FURTHER READING

GENERAL

Beard, T. C., and Gray, W. R., *Handbook for the Canberra Blood Pressure Trial*, 1983. An informative handbook about salt and sodium for the participants of the Canberra Blood Pressure Trial in 1983.

Briggs, D., and Wahlqvist, M., *Food Facts*, Penguin Books Australia: Ringwood, 1984. A factual book, interestingly presented, giving information on the nutrients in a wide range of foods.

Commonwealth Department of Health, *Towards Better Nutrition for Australians: Report of the Nutrition Taskforce of the Better Health Commission*, Australian Government Publishing Service: Canberra, 1987. A report on diet and nutrition in Australia.

Denton, D., *The Hunger for Salt*, Springer-Verlag: Berlin, 1984. A comprehensive book on physiological and other aspects of sodium.

Hanssen, M., with Marsden, J. *Additive Code Breaker*, Lothian: Melbourne, 1986. A reference book deciphering the codes of food additives. Revised for Australia by the Commonwealth Department of Health.

BIOCHEMISTRY OF COOKING

Berk, Z., *Braverman's Introduction to the Biochemistry of Foods*, Elsevier Scientific: New York, 1976.

McGee, H., *On Food and Cooking*, Allen & Unwin: London, 1986.

HEALTHY EATING

Burkitt, D., *Don't Forget Fibre in your Diet*, Collins: Sydney, 1980. A book in which the scientific evidence of the value of fibre in our diet is clearly presented.

Commonwealth Department of Health, *Dietary Guidelines for Australians*, Australian Government Publishing Service: Canberra, 1986.

Guide to Healthy Eating, The National Heart Foundation of Australia, 1982. An authoritative book with recipes and advice on diet.

Planning Fat-controlled Meals, The National Heart Foundation of Australia.

COOKERY AND FOOD

Mrs Beeton's Cookery and Household Management, Ward Lock: London, 12th impression, 1972. A book that has stood the test of time with excellent and reliable recipes, and sound advice on cooking.

Goode, J., *The World Guide to Cooking with Fruit and Vegetables*, Macmillan Company of Australia: Melbourne, 1973. This book provides a comprehensive account of fruits, vegetables, herbs and spices, and contains an excellent chart of the most common herbs and spices and the vegetables they match.

Grigson, J. (contributing editor), *The World Atlas of Food*, Mitchell Beazley: London, 1974. This book provides a wealth of information on many aspects of food.

SLOW-COOKING TECHNIQUE

Atterbury, S., *Leave it to Cook*, Penguin Books: Harmondsworth, England, 1978. This book is informative about the technique of long, slow cooking.

HERBS AND SPICES

Loewenfeld, C., and Back, P., *Herbs for Health and Cookery*, Pan Books: London, 1977.

Lust, J., *The Herb Book*, Bantam Books: New York, 1974.

Stobart, T., *Herbs, Spices and Flavourings*, Penguin Books: Harmondsworth, England, 1977.

REGIONAL COOKERY

Fitzgibbon, T., *A Taste of Wales*, Pan Books: London, 1973.

Gööck, R., *Das neue grosse Kochbuch*, Bertelsmann Ratgeberverlag: Gütersloh, 1970.

Hosain, A., and Pasricha, S., *Cooking the Indian Way*, Sun Books: Melbourne; Hamlyn Publishing Group: Feltham, England, 1969.

Lo, K., *Chinese Food*, Penguin Books: Harmondsworth, England, 1974.

Philippou, M. J., *101 Arabian Delights*, Clifton Books: Brighton, England, 1969.

Roden, C., *A Book of Middle Eastern Food*, Penguin Books: Harmondsworth, England, 1974.

COOKERY OF SPECIFIC FOODS

Elliot, R., *The Bean Book*, Fontana/Collins: Glasgow, 1979.

Grigson, J., *Fish Cookery*, Penguin Books: Harmondsworth, England, 1975.

INDEX OF RECIPES

SUCCULENT SEAFOOD IDEAS

VERSATILE VEGETABLES AND RICE

MAINSTAY MEAT AND CHICKEN

SALADS WITH A GREAT FLAVOUR

GENERAL INDEX

This index does not include recipes, but it does occasionally refer to subjects discussed within them. It also refers to information given in italics at the top of some pages. For a comprehensive listing of recipe titles, turn to the Index of Recipes (pp. 187–191).

allspice 17, 26, 27, 28
aniseed 17, 26, 170
apple mint 170

baking powder 7, 170, 172
basil 15, 17, 27, 28, 31, 136
bay 17, 26, 27, 28, 31
beans, herbs and spices
  with 26
biscuits, herbs and spices
  with 26
blood pressure v, viii, 1, 2, 3, 5,
  12, 48, 122
borage 27
bread 11
  breadcrumbs 41, 127
  herbs and spices with 26
  tips on preparing 158, 165
  to 'punch down' dough 158
  toast 38
butter 6

cabbage 15
cakes, herbs and spices
  with 26, 170
calcium oxalate 5
Canberra Blood Pressure Trial
  (1983) xi, 1–2, 4
capers 28
capsicum 15
caraway 17, 26, 27, 28
cardamom 17, 26, 170
cardiovascular disease v
carrot 15
casseroles, herbs and spices
  with 26
celery seeds 18, 26, 28, 30, 31
cereals 11–12, 34
cheese (low sodium) 6, 12,
  112, 120, 150
chervil 18, 28, 30, 31
chicken 140
  breasts 142
  cuts for stock or
    casseroles 63
  roasting times 136
chilli 18, 26, 27, 28, 31
chives 15, 18, 27, 28, 30
cholesterol 6
cinnamon 18, 26, 27, 28, 170
cloves 19, 26, 27, 28, 170
coconut milk 6, 95, 120
common salt see sodium:
  sodium chloride
cooking salt see sodium:
  sodium chloride
coriander 26, 27, 28, 31